Gay & Lesbian Medical Rights

Gay & Lesbian Medical Rights

How to Protect Yourself, Your Partner, and Your Family

Brette McWhorter Sember,
Author of *The Complete Gay Divorce*

CAREER PRESS
Franklin Lakes, N.J.

GAY & LESBIAN MEDICAL RIGHTS
EDITED AND TYPESET BY GINA TALUCCI
Cover design by Mada Design, Inc. / NYC
Printed in the U.S.A. by Book-mart Press

To order this title, please call toll-free 1-800-CAREER-1 (NJ and Canada: 201-848-0310) to order using VISA or MasterCard, or for further information on books from Career Press.

The Career Press, Inc., 3 Tice Road, PO Box 687,
Franklin Lakes, NJ 07417
www.careerpress.com

Library of Congress Cataloging-in-Publication Data

Sember, Brette McWhorter, 1968-
    Gay & lesbian medical rights : how to protect yourself, your partner, and your family / by Brette McWhorter Sember.
        p. cm.
    ISBN-13: 978-1-56414-896-4
    ISBN-10: 1-56414-896-4
        1. Medical care--Law and legislation--United States. 2. Gay couples--Legal status, laws, etc.--United States. 3. Gay rights--United States. 4. Children of gay parents--Legal status, laws, etc.--United States. I. Title. II. Title: Gay and lesbian medical rights.

KF3823.S46 2006
344.7304′ 1--dc22
                                                                                    2006011946

Contents

Introduction

Personal health is probably the most basic component of a happy life. Being healthy is the basis for all of life's other activities. When you're ill, it is difficult to be happy, focused, or satisfied about anything else in your life. Illness can also often be an expensive proposition—not to mention an emotionally challenging one.

When you are healthy, all the "what ifs" may not seem to be relevant or important, but it is the best time to consider your situation and make plans for the future. Coping with medical issues is a complicated and troublesome concern for anyone, but for members of the gay and lesbian community, things become exponentially difficult. Basic rights become questionable.

- Can I see my partner while he is in the hospital?
- Can I get health insurance for my stay-at-home partner?
- What steps must I take to enable my partner to make health care decisions for me if I'm unable to?
- Can I get time off to spend with our new child?
- Can I be discriminated against because I have HIV?

While it is true that laws are slowly evolving, allowing more rights to gay couples, changes are not happening rapidly enough or widely enough to offer the many protections and rights that are needed. Because of this, if you want to protect yourself and your family, you have no choice but to do so on your own. That means understanding what your options are and what steps you can take to duplicate the rights of heterosexual couples, or to protect your rights as a single gay person.

This book is your guide to the complicated and confusing questions facing you. Each chapter takes you through an issue and offers the possible solutions available to you. Many of the situations discussed in this book may not be issues confronting you now, such as end of life issues or terminal illnesses. No one wants to think about these kinds of issues, but, in order to plan for the future and protect yourself, your partner, and your children, it is essential that you think about and talk about these scenarios now, so that you can develop a plan, and the necessary documentation, should you ever find yourself in that situation. The time to make those decisions is when you have the luxury of good health and the time to consider them carefully. In the middle of a medical crisis, you don't want to worry about making decisions and executing documents you have no prior experience with.

This book is meant to be one of hope, and, although it does include information about difficult topics, it is meant to serve as a source of information. I hope this book arms you with the knowledge that allows you to make decisions that are right for you and helps you work through some of the decisions you are facing.

Choosing to be proactive about your health rights is a decision that will be worth the time and effort. Many people feel more comfortable after they have put into place the necessary protections and chosen their options. Health care decisions should be things you take time to consider, and then move past. Nothing in this book should keep you up at night or make you worry. Instead, use the solutions you find here to make your life, and your partner's or family's, easier and happier.

This book is as up to date as possible, but because laws are always changing, it is always important to consult an attorney in your state to understand your rights as they currently stand. Also, a book is never a substitute for personal legal advice, so you should always see an attorney about your own situation. It is also essential that you use the correct state forms for things such as health care directives, powers of attorney, and other documents, so that there will be no question of whether the document is accepted in your state. The forms provided in this book are for example purposes *only* and are not intended to be used and should not be relied upon, because the forms required in each state are different.

This publication is designed to provide accurate and authoritative information in regard to the subject matter covered. It is sold with the understanding that the publisher or author is not engaged in rendering legal, accounting, or other professional services. If legal advice or other expert assistance is required, the services of a competent professional person should be sought. This book is not a substitute for legal advice.

Here's to your health!

Chapter 1

Knowledge Is Power:

Understanding Your Rights

Understanding your rights is the first step towards becoming a wise medical services consumer. The most important thing you need to know is that you have the absolute right to make informed, educated decisions about your own health. Decisions about your health should be made by you after you have received input from medical professionals you trust. It is too easy these days to feel as if you are adrift in the system and that your fate is decided by others. It is essential that you take control of your own life and medical choices.

The fact that you are gay, lesbian, bisexual, or transgendered (GLBT) should have no impact on your ability to receive good medical care and make your own medical decisions;

unfortunately we know that, right now, it does frequently have an impact. Realizing this is the first step to taking control of your own situation.

Discrimination

Discrimination against gays and lesbians is still a pervasive problem in medical care; discrimination can take on many forms. A physician or hospital may refuse to treat a GLBT patient. Health care workers may treat a GLBT patient differently, or feel less inclined to follow privacy laws. Treatments can be withheld or denied. Insurance companies may scrutinize claims more closely. In short, there are many ways that discrimination can occur in the health care field. Recognizing it is the first step. Doing something about it is another.

While many physicians provide excellent care to patients regardless of sexual identity, some physicians say they do not wish to treat gay or lesbian patients because it conflicts with their own moral or religious beliefs. Others are simply uncomfortable and have no idea how to provide care in a fair and reasonable way. This kind of reaction would seem to undermine the basic oath and premise involved in being a physician, but some do not see it this way. Michigan passed a law in 2004 called the Conscientious Objector Policy Act, which allows health care professionals to refuse to treat a gay or lesbian patient if the provider has a moral or ethical objection. A health care provider must object, in writing, to providing a specific type of health care (the act also allows physicians to refuse to prescribe contraceptives, so it does not target gays alone), and provide it to his or her employer. However, the provider cannot refuse to give treatment in an emergency situation.

California has made important inroads in preventing health care discrimination against gays and lesbians. A case (*Benitez v. North Coast Women's Care Medical Group*) held that California doctors in for-profit groups must not discriminate against patients based upon sexual orientation. The case specifically dealt with infertility treatment for a lesbian, but the court decision applies to all medical care for gays and lesbians.

The following states have laws that prohibit discrimination in medical care:

- California
- Connecticut
- Hawaii
- Illinois
- Maine
- Maryland
- Massachusetts
- Minnesota
- New Hampshire
- New Jersey
- New Mexico
- New York
- Rhode Island
- Wisconsin
- Vermont
- Washington, D.C.

There are also some municipalities and counties that have local laws as well. It is important to note that organizations such as the American Medical Association (AMA) and American College of Obstetricians and Gynecologists (ACOG) have adopted statements that make it clear that physicians should not discriminate against patients based on sexual orientation.

Discrimination in medical care can have many faces and applications, from blatant refusal to treat a gay patient, to a lack of respect or compassion in dealings with a gay patient, to failure to treat HIV positive patients with the same standard as other patients, as well as more subtle discrimination the provider may not even be aware of. Recently a Florida woman saw her doctor for bronchitis and when she left the office she was handed pamphlets and information on gay conversion therapy. The Florida State Department of Health is currently investigating. This kind of treatment is harassment, not to mention medically unsound. The American Medical Association, the American Psychiatric Association, the American Academy of Pediatrics, the American Counseling Association, the American Psychological Association, the National Association of School Psychologists, and the National Association of Social Workers all reject gay conversion therapy.

If you encounter discrimination, it is your choice how to handle it. Some people wish to avoid a confrontation. Others feel nothing will happen if they personally do not seek change.

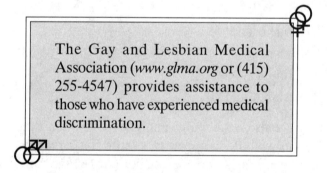

The Gay and Lesbian Medical Association (*www.glma.org* or (415) 255-4547) provides assistance to those who have experienced medical discrimination.

If you have experienced discrimination in health care and want to take action, there are several things you can do. First, determine if the health care provider's institution or practice has a policy on discrimination and if so, send a letter detailing your experiences. Report the health care provider to the state licensing board for unprofessional behavior. If your state or locality has an anti-discrimination law that covers medical care, contact your state attorney general to file a report. Let other members of your community know. And most importantly of all, find another health care provider. The Gay and Lesbian Medical Association (*www.glma.org*) has an online referral program you can use to locate a gay-friendly provider. If you were referred to this provider by your primary care doctor, let him or her know about the treatment you received so that he or she can stop making referrals to this provider. If you received treatment by a nurse, physician's assistant, aide, or staff member in a doctor's office that was discriminatory, let your main provider in that office know about it.

Informed Consent

One of the basis tenets of medical care is the patient's right to make decisions for him- or herself. In our medical system, all patients have the right to informed consent, a policy that means as a patient, you must be informed about all the risks and benefits of any surgery, test, medication, or other medical procedure before you agree. A patient who is not aware of all of these factors cannot make a fully informed decision. You also have the right to refuse any medical care you don't want. It's your body and you have the right to decide what will happen to it.

Unfortunately, informed consent is very often not obtained in day-to-day medical care. For example, has anyone ever explained the possible risks of a simple blood test or discussed the long-term impact of radiation from an X ray with you? It's highly unlikely. There is an assumption that, as patients, we have basic medical information. This assumption often extends to medical care that is beyond basic as well. Because of this, the onus is on patients to make sure they ask the right questions, do their own research, and never take anything for granted. Some health care providers simply assume consent without really obtaining it. You always have the right to get information, to ask questions, or to discuss other options.

There are some providers who become annoyed or who have little tolerance for patients who come in with lists of questions and copies of studies they have downloaded from the Internet, but as a patient, you have the absolute right to ask all of your questions and consider all possibilities before you make any kind of decision. If you are with a provider who is not willing to afford you that opportunity, you should find someone who will listen to your questions and concerns and help you come to an informed decision. There are also some providers who don't intend to be quick or incomplete in their explanations, but find that many patients do not ask for detailed information. If you want more information, you have a right to it.

The power to make medical decisions must be in your hands. Your health care provider is there to provide information and opinions—he or she cannot (and should not) make choices for you. A health care provider who fails to inform you of risks can be civilly liable for performing a procedure without you fully agreeing to the possible risks.

Second Opinions

A second opinion can be a valuable tool in helping you evaluate your treatment options, diagnosis, and overall health care. Second opinions are generally covered by health insurance, but call to find out just to be sure. When seeking a second opinion, it is usually best not to ask the first doctor for a recommendation. You want someone with a completely different perspective and, if you get a referral, you'll probably be sent to someone who agrees with your first doctor.

Blood and Sperm Donations

At the current time, men who have sex with other men are not permitted to donate blood or bone marrow because of an FDA prohibition. There is a lot of movement towards changing this policy, because blood can now be evaluated for HIV and hepatitis more quickly and thoroughly, but it has yet to be altered. Women who have sex with other women are not banned from donations as long as they meet other criteria. (See *www.redcross.org* for more information on blood donation requirements.)

Men who have had sex with men within the last five years are not permitted to donate sperm to a sperm bank. If a private donation is made, gay donors are not specifically banned, however some clinics will refuse to do insemination with sperm from an admittedly gay male. If this is something you are interested in, check the clinic's policies before naming a donor.

Clinical Trials

If you are diagnosed with a medical condition that doesn't have a cure as of yet, you may be searching for answers and alternatives. Often there are ongoing clinical trials of new medications or treatments that may be beneficial to you. Everyone has the right to consider and pursue these types of treatments. Finding out about new trials is easier than ever. Complete listings of trials in the United States are available at *www.clinicaltrials.gov* and international trials are available at *www.centerwatch.com*. Clinical trials allow you to access medication or treatments that have not yet been approved, however, you must be aware that most studies are double blind studies, in which neither you nor the health care provider knows if you are receiving the actual medication or a placebo. For many people though, taking a chance on a clinical trial is better than sitting and waiting for a treatment to be approved.

Addiction Treatment

The abuse of alcohol and crystal meth among gay men is widely considered as a central element to the spreading of HIV (because impaired judgment affects condom use). There are no statistics available about gay and lesbian alcohol and drug abuse, but it is considered to be higher than rates in the general population. Of gay men, 41.5 percent report tobacco use, compared with 26.6 percent of all men in general. Twice as many lesbian women smoke in comparison with all women. Alcohol and drug use is highest among young gays and lesbians (opposite of the general population, where alcohol use increases with age), but gay men and lesbian women of all ages report that they have alcohol problems nearly twice as often as the general population. Addiction is an ongoing health concern for the GLBT community.

In addition to the dangers of the drugs themselves, a recent study found that crystal meth users are three times as likely to be infected with HIV. Other drugs and substances can have the same impact because they loosen inhibitions and make unprotected sex more likely.

Seeking treatment for addiction is difficult, but worth the effort. If you decide to seek treatment, The National Association of Gay and Lesbian Addiction Professionals can provide information and referrals at *www.nalgap.org* or (703) 465-0539 for information on how to find a professional who is experienced in working with GLBT clients. You can also ask your primary physician for a recommendation or check your local Lavender Pages for experienced addiction counselors in your area. Addiction treatment is often covered under most health insurance plans, but you should check to see how much coverage you have and if there are co-pays and caps.

Eating Disorders

There is a perception that eating disorders are a problem that young women in general face; few recognize this as a gay issue. However, approximately 20 percent of males with eating disorders are believed to be gay; this is a highly unrecognized fact. Eating disorders are a serious health risk and stem from self-esteem problems and control issues. Getting help with an eating disorder is essential, because they are very difficult to overcome. When men face eating disorders, it is not usually through pursuit of being thin, but instead is a quest to be fit, lean, and muscular. Often, weight loss stems from excessive exercise. It is important to note that AIDS wasting is not the same as an eating disorder and these conditions should not be grouped together or treated in the same way. Eating disorder treatment is normally covered by insurance, although in-patient treatment may have specific caps and co-pays.

For information about eating disorders, or to find a treatment provider, contact The National Eating Disorders Association at *www.eatingdisorders.org* or (800) 931-2237.

Domestic Violence

Even within the GLBT community, people may not recognize that domestic violence is not only a heterosexual problem. Same sex couples face domestic violence as well, and it is often a greater problem than for heterosexual couples because there is very little help available and very little public knowledge of the problem. Domestic violence is about more than physical violence though, and usually involves mental or emotional violence and threats. Among gay couples, the threat of outing a partner is sometimes used as a part of other violence. An article in the *American Bar Association Journal* in 1998 reported that 25–33 percent of gay couples experience domestic violence. An article in the *Valparaiso University Law Review* in 1995 reported that between 50,000 and 100,000 lesbian women and as many as 500,000 gay men have experienced domestic violence. The Gay Men's Domestic Violence Project did a survey of more than 2,000 men at the 1997 Boston Pride event, finding that 25 percent of gay men have experienced domestic violence.

It is illegal to physically harm another person, so you can always seek protection and assistance if you are physically harmed by a partner. This is complicated by the fact that some law enforcement officers are reluctant to get involved in domestic disputes; this reluctance is increased when the people involved are gay or lesbian. Some law enforcement officers simply have not been educated about domestic violence in the gay community, while others may have personal prejudices. Sometimes, there is even the shocking perception that when domestic violence occurs within a gay relationship that it must be mutual or consensual.

Domestic violence laws impose harsher punishments than regular assault and battery laws (because you're in a relationship, it enhances your responsibility to each other). Many domestic violence laws not only allow victims to obtain restraining orders (see page 28), but also to retain exclusive possession of a residence for a certain period of time without the other party being granted an opportunity to appear in court.

The first step to getting help with this kind of problem is recognizing that there is a problem. If you are in an abusive relationship, you need to create a safety plan that will allow you to get out. If you have children, the safety of your children must also be a prime consideration. For many people, family and friends are the first line of help and support in this kind of situation.

If you find yourself in a position of abuse, your first step in an emergency is to call the police. Even if you are not treated respectfully, this presents an opportunity to temporarily stop the abuse and gives you a chance to get away.

Domestic violence shelters are an important resource for many, but unfortunately they may not be willing to accept gays or lesbians. These shelters are traditionally for women who suffer violence at the hands of men. While many shelters do understand that domestic violence involves same-sex couples similar to heterosexual couples, there are others that may be run by church groups or who simply take a more conservative approach. Going to a shelter may put you in the position of needing to explain you are gay or lie about the sex of your abuser. But if you can get to a shelter, it is likely they will help you, or at least tell you where to go to get help. Domestic violence shelters do not publicize their locations, so to contact them, you must do so by phone.

There are several ways to find a domestic violence shelter. If you call 911 they can tell you who to contact. You can also call the National Domestic Violence Hotline at (800) 799-7233 or visit them online at *www.ndvh.org*. The site includes a list of state domestic violence coalitions available at *www.ncadv.org/resources/state.htm*. If you locate the one for your state and call them, they can tell you where to find GLBT domestic violence assistance in your area.

For more information on domestic violence, visit *http:// gaynorfolk-net.norfolk.on.ca/life-on-brians-beat/samesexviolence.html* or *www.rainbowdomesticviolence.itgo.com.*

Once you have gotten out of an abusive situation, you have the right to seek a restraining order against your abuser—but for same-sex couples, Delaware, Montana, and South Carolina do not allow restraining orders. Restraining orders will direct your abuser to stay away from you (often a distance will be specified). A restraining order is also a very important piece of paper to have because if your abuser should return, the order requires the police to take action against him or her. It enhances your believability. There are no restrictions on who may seek a restraining order, but most laws are written to include people who live together (which would include domestic partners). In 18 states, the laws do not provide protection to people who do not live together, so couples who are dating are not covered.

To seek a restraining order, you will need to appear at your local family or criminal court. Some jurisdictions classify domestic violence cases so that they are heard in both courts simultaneously making sure all aspects of the case are dealt with; but some states do not include gay cases in the jurisdiction of family court. You can file a petition on your own, or you can seek help from a law enforcement office or a domestic violence shelter worker.

As if there aren't enough dangers in domestic violence matters, a primary concern is that many victims try to defend themselves and end up getting charged with a crime. Or in rare cases, a judge may not take the time to understand the situation, and may punish the victim while letting the batterer go free.

If you have children and your child is being abused by your partner, call 911 or report the situation to your state child abuse hotline (located in the government guide in your phone book). You can also call the National Child Abuse Hotline at (800) 422-4453 or access a list of state phone numbers online at *www.childhelp.com/report_local.htm*.

Suicide

The National Institute of Mental Health does not have national statistics available about all suicide rates. Gays and lesbians do not appear to have a higher suicide rate than other people, although some studies have shown that gay teens are at a higher risk—at the very least they report a higher number of suicidal thoughts as well as suicide attempts. However, transgender individuals have an extremely high rate of suicide: 35 percent of transgender patients contemplate suicide and 16 percent actually attempt suicide. These statistics only include TG individuals who are seeking treatment of some kind—there are many more who have no contact with the medical establishment. Because of the increased risks for teens and TGs, suicide is an important issue for the gay and lesbian community. For information about physician-assisted suicide, see Chapter 7.

> If you or someone you know is contemplating suicide, you can get help at these hotlines: 1-800-SUI-CIDE or 1-800-273-TALK. State hotlines can also be found online at *www.suicidehotlines.com*.

Hepatitis Vaccines

Hepatitis is a confusing and dangerous illness. There are three types: A, B, and C. Hepatitis can be spread by sexual contact (as well as other methods) and is part of the STD group. Vaccines for A and B strains prevent the disease. (Hepatitis A and B are the only STDs that are preventable by vaccines.) The CDC recommends hepatitis B vaccines for all adults and hepatitis A vaccines for men who have sex with men, as well as people in some other risk categories. If you have not been vaccinated, you can ask your health care provider about the vaccine and specific recommendations for you. The vaccine is an important step you can take to protect your health, but unfortunately it is not something that health care providers often suggest unless a patient is openly gay or has other risk factors. The vaccine is covered by health insurance plans.

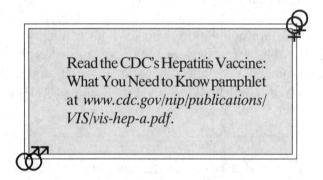

Read the CDC's Hepatitis Vaccine: What You Need to Know pamphlet at *www.cdc.gov/nip/publications/ VIS/vis-hep-a.pdf*.

Mental Health Care

Should you, or you and a partner, decide that you want to obtain counseling or therapy, it is important to choose a therapist you are comfortable with and who is experienced in GLBT issues.

You can ask family and friends for referrals, as well as your primary care physician. When selecting a therapist, ask questions on the phone and try to get a feeling as to whether this is a person with whom you would be comfortable.

If you and a partner are seeking relationship or marriage therapy, be sure to ask if the therapist has worked with gay couples before. You want someone who is familiar with gay relationships and has successfully worked in that kind of situation before.

> If you need help locating a mental health professional experienced in GLBT issues, contact the Gay and Lesbian International Therapist Search Engine (GLITSE) at *www.glitse.com*. The Association of Gay and Lesbian Psychiatrists provides referrals as well and can be contacted at *www.aglp.org* or (215) 222-2800.

Mental health care is covered by most insurance plans (but always check first because there are often co-pays and a cap on the number of visits per year) and is simply another aspect of health care that can make a big improvement in your life. If you and a partner seek relationship or marriage therapy and you have separate insurance plans, you should call in advance and ask the therapist if he or she will be able to bill the entire amount to one insurance company, or if it will need to be billed to both companies in some kind of apportioned way. It is important to know what kind of mental health coverage you each have before you make contact.

If you ever encounter a therapist or mental health worker who tries to tell you being gay is a mental health illness, something you can change, or something you need to alter, find someone else. Unfortunately there are still some homophobic mental health professionals.

For information on Gender Identity Disorder (GID) or Gender Identity Dysphoria, the technical mental health terms for the situations of transgender individuals, see Chapter 10.

Same-Sex Unions and Your Medical Rights

If you and your partner have entered into a same-sex marriage or civil union, you are afforded the same rights as married couples, but only in the states which recognize these unions. In the state in which you were married or unioned, and in states that recognize the union, you are considered next of kin and can make medical decisions for each other. You also have the right to visit your partner in the hospital (see Chapter 6 for more information about hospital visitation policies) without any difficulties.

Unfortunately, you may not be afforded these rights in states that do not recognize gay unions, although it is always best to act as if you are entitled to these rights than to ask permission. Use the word "spouse" and people may respond better. If you live in a different state than the state you got your union or marriage in, your current state of residence probably does not recognize your union and you will need to take the necessary steps to protect your rights under your state laws.

An interesting note is that getting hitched could actually be good for your health, as well as your love life. Studies show that married heterosexuals are healthier than single people (showing benefits in cardiovascular health as well as overall happiness and well-being), and a study in the British *Journal of Epidemiology and Community Health* concluded that it is likely the same benefits exist for same-sex couples. Further supporting this, the American Psychiatric Association issued a statement in 2005 saying that that same-sex marriage "maintains and supports" mental health.

Chapter 2

Make Your Voice Heard:

Health Care Directives

Making your own decisions about medical care is a basic right. Part of this right is the ability to decide what kind of care you are unwilling to accept, as well as who you want to make decisions for you should you become unable to. Through the use of legal documents called health care directives, you can make these choices and be certain they will be followed. The key to these types of documents is planning ahead and creating them before you think you might need them. No one wants to think about a time when they might not be able to make their own decisions or about a time when life-sustaining treatment might be discontinued; as a result a lot of people never discuss their wishes with their loved ones. Making the effort to talk about these difficult subjects can ease everyone's mind and give you the sense that you've done what you can to protect each other in the future.

Why You Need a Health Care Directive

A health care directive (also called an advance directive) is a written document that specifies the types of medical treatments you do not wish to receive and also specifies who you want to make medical decisions for you when you are unable to. If you do not have a valid health care directive, decisions about your medical care will be made by your next of kin. If you are not legally joined with a partner in the eyes of your state, next of kin will be your parents or siblings (or adult children). Even if you are confident that your family members would make the right choices, it makes their job easier if you have spelled out your wishes. There is no wondering and no angst about what to do. If you want your partner to be the one to make decisions for you and your state does not recognize your commitment to each other, an advance directive is essential.

You must be 18 years of age and of "sound mind" to execute a valid health care directive. Even if you and your partner live in a state that recognizes your union and gives you the right to make medical decisions for each other, you still need to execute these documents so that if you travel or need to be transferred for specialty medical care they are in place.

Rights if You Are Partnered

If you and your partner have married, or obtained a civil union or domestic partnership in your state, you already have some rights to make decisions for each other. But it is still important to execute a document expressing your wishes and appointing your partner as your decision-maker in case you become ill in another state or if laws in your state change. Following are current rights:

- ✚ **Massachusetts:** Married same sex couples have the same rights as married couples to make health care decisions for each other within the state.

- ✚ **Vermont and Connecticut:** Couples with civil unions have the same rights as married couples to make health care decisions within the state.

- ✚ **Maine:** Domestic partners have priority over family members to act as a guardian if the partner becomes disabled within the state.

- ✚ **New Jersey and California:** Domestic partners have the right to make medical decisions for each other within the state.

Talking About Your Wishes

Talking about your wishes is an important step in the process. Before you discuss your wishes with anyone though, the first thing you need to do is think about what your wishes are. This can be difficult because this isn't the kind of thing most people like to think about. Because of the wide range of medical treatments available today, there are many, many possibilities for life-continuing treatment. You need to consider what kind of treatment you would want and what kind you would not want (for example, ventilators, restarting your heart, feeding tubes, and so on). Telling yourself it won't happen to you or that it is so far off in the future that you don't need to think about it is not helpful. We never know when illness or injury will strike, so it is always best to plan for the worst but hope for the best.

Once you have reached some decisions about what is right for you, it is important to talk to your family, partner, and loved ones about your feelings. If you are going to designate a person to make these decisions for you, many states require that you have already discussed your wishes in advance with the person you name. Also, you want to make sure everyone in your immediate family knows and understands your wishes clearly, so that there won't be fighting over making certain decisions. You want there to be no question that you have made up your mind. It's also important to take the time to make sure that the people in your life not only know your wishes but really understand why you've made the choices that you have.

Types of Documents

There are several different types of legal documents about health care, and the one you use will depend mainly on what the standard is in your state. Different states call these different things, so the terms used in this book may not be the ones your state uses. It is best to consult an attorney in your state so that you get the maximum protection by using forms that are accepted by courts in your state.

Living Wills

A living will is a type of health care directive that describes your wishes about life-saving or life-sustaining medical care, should you become terminally ill or in a permanent vegetative state. It is sometimes called a "declaration regarding life-prolonging procedures" or a "declaration." The document is very specific and lists exactly what kinds of care you do not want to receive, such as:

- Surgery.
- CPR.
- Antibiotics.
- Kidney dialysis.
- Respirator or ventilator.
- Food and water through tubes.
- Chemotherapy.
- Blood transfusions.

It can also offer specific instruction about the type of pain management you wish to receive (some pain medication can worsen a condition, so you need to be specific about them), as well as hospice care, at-home care, maximum pain relief, and so on. To obtain a living will, you need to have an attorney create one for you and make sure it fulfills your state's requirements because these documents tend to be extremely detailed and lengthy.

You can view a sample living will at *www.euthanasia.com/lw.html*.

Health Care Proxy

A health care proxy (also sometimes called a health care power of attorney) is a more simplified document that names the person you have selected to make medical decisions for you should you become unable to do so, and also may provide very basic instruction about the kind of care you do not wish to receive. The person you choose to make decisions for you is called your proxy. It is always a good idea to also select an alternate proxy in case the first proxy is not available. It is also important to tell your proxy you want to name him or her so that this authority does not come as a surprise.

Your proxy will have the right to:

- ✚ Talk to doctors about your care.
- ✚ Access and obtain copies of all of your medical records.
- ✚ Choose what providers and facilities will provide care for you.
- ✚ Refuse treatment.
- ✚ Seek second opinions.
- ✚ Choose alternative or holistic treatments.
- ✚ Make any and all decisions about your health, whether you have specifically spelled them out or not.
- ✚ Visit you in the hospital or care facility.
- ✚ Get a court to enforce your wishes if your physicians will not.

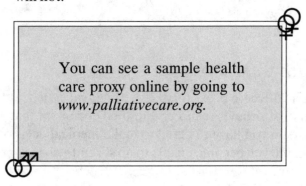

You can see a sample health care proxy online by going to *www.palliativecare.org.*

Advance Directive

An advance directive is a document that combines the aspects of both living wills and health care proxies. This document describes the types of treatment you would not want and also designates a person to make decisions for you should you be unable to do so. Your attorney will be able to create a document that fulfills your state's requirements, but it is important to know that all states are required to respect a patient's clear wishes, based on the famous Nancy Cruzan Supreme Court case. Following is a sample form for a health care directive.

You can download state specific forms online at *www.uslivingwillregistry.com/ forms.shtm*.

ADVANCE HEALTH CARE DIRECTIVE
(California Probate Code Section 4701)
Explanation

You have the right to give instructions about your own health care. You also have the right to name someone else to make health care decisions for you. This form lets you do either or both of these things. It also lets you express your wishes regarding donation of organs and the designation of your primary physician. If you use this form, you may complete or modify all or any part of it. You are free to use a different form.

Part 1 of this form is a power of attorney for health care. Part 1 lets you name another individual as agent to make health care decisions for you if you become incapable of making your own decisions or if you want someone else to make those decisions for you now even though you are still capable. You may also name an alternate agent to act for you if your first choice is not willing, able, or reasonably available to make decisions for you. (Your agent may not be an operator or employee of a community care facility or a residential care facility where you are receiving care, or your supervising health care provider or employee of the health care institution where you are receiving care, unless your agent is related to you or is a coworker.)

Unless the form you sign limits the authority of your agent, your agent may make all health care decisions for you. This form has a place for you to limit the authority of your agent. You need not limit the authority of your agent if you wish to rely on your agent for all health care decisions that may have to be made. If you choose not to limit the authority of your agent, your agent will have the right to:

(a) Consent or refuse consent to any care, treatment, service, or procedure to maintain, diagnose, or otherwise affect a physical or mental condition.

(b) Select or discharge health care providers and institutions.

(c) Approve or disapprove diagnostic tests, surgical procedures, and programs of medication.

(d) Direct the provision, withholding, or withdrawal of artificial nutrition and hydration and all other forms of health care, including cardiopulmonary resuscitation. (e) Make anatomical gifts, authorize an autopsy, and direct disposition of remains. Part 2 of this form lets you give specific instructions about any aspect of your health care, whether or not you appoint an agent. Choices are provided for you to express your wishes regarding the provision, withholding, or withdrawal of treatment to keep you alive, as well as the provision of pain relief. Space is also provided for you to add to the choices you have made or for you to write out any additional wishes. If you are satisfied to allow your agent to determine what is best for you in making end-of-life decisions, you need not fill out Part 2 of this form.

Part 3 of this form lets you express an intention to donate your bodily organs and tissues following your death.

Part 4 of this form lets you designate a physician to have primary responsibility for your health care.

After completing this form, sign and date the form at the end. The form must be signed by two qualified witnesses or acknowledged before a notary public. Give a copy of the signed and completed form to your physician, to any other health care providers you may have, to any health care institution at which you are receiving care, and to any health care agents you have named. You should talk to the person you have named as agent to make sure that he or she understands your wishes and is willing to take the responsibility.

You have the right to revoke this advance health care directive or replace this form at any time.

PART 1
POWER OF ATTORNEY FOR HEALTH CARE

(1.1) DESIGNATION OF AGENT: I designate the following individual as my agent to make health care decisions for me:

_____

(name of individual you choose as agent)

_____

(address)   (city)   (state)   (ZIP Code)

_____

(home phone)   (work phone)

OPTIONAL: If I revoke my agent's authority or if my agent is not willing, able, or reasonably available to make a health care decision for me, designate as my first alternate agent:

_____

(name of individual you choose as first alternate agent)

_____

(address)   (city)   (state)   (ZIP Code)

_____

(home phone)   (work phone)

OPTIONAL: If I revoke the authority of my agent and first alternate agent or if neither is willing, able, or reasonably available to make a health care decision for me, I designate as my second alternate agent:

_____

(name of individual you choose as second alternate agent)

_____

(address)   (city)   (state)   (ZIP Code)

_____

(home phone)   (work phone)

(1.2) AGENT'S AUTHORITY: My agent is authorized to make all health care decisions for me, including decisions to provide, withhold, or withdraw artificial nutrition and hydration and all other forms of health care to keep me alive, except as I state here:

_____
_____
_____

(Add additional sheets if needed.)

(1.3) WHEN AGENT'S AUTHORITY BECOMES EFFECTIVE: My agent's authority becomes effective when my primary physician determines that I am unable to make my own health care decisions unless I mark the following box. If I mark this box (), my agent's authority to make health care decisions for me takes effect immediately.

(1.4) AGENT'S OBLIGATION: My agent shall make health care decisions for me in accordance with this power of attorney for health care, any instructions I give in Part 2 of this form, and my other wishes to the extent known to my agent. To the extent my wishes are unknown, my agent shall make health care decisions for me in accordance with what my agent determines to be in my best interest. In determining my best interest, my agent shall consider my personal values to the extent known to my agent.

(1.5) AGENT'S POSTDEATH AUTHORITY: My agent is authorized to make anatomical gifts, authorize an autopsy, and direct disposition of my remains, except as I state here or in Part 3 of this form:

_____
_____
_____

(Add additional sheets if needed.)

(1.6) NOMINATION OF CONSERVATOR: If a conservator of my person needs to be appointed for me by a court, I nominate the agent designated inthis form. If that agent is not willing, able, or reasonably available to act as conservator, I nominate the alternate agents whom I have named, in the order designated.

PART 2

INSTRUCTIONS FOR HEALTH CARE

If you fill out this part of the form, you may strike any wording you do not want.

(2.1) END-OF-LIFE DECISIONS: I direct that my health care providers and others involved in my care provide, withhold, or withdral treatment inaccordance with the choice I have marked below:

(a) Choice Not To Prolong Life

I do not want my life to be prolonged if (1) I have an incurable and irreversible condition that will result in my death within a relatively short time, (2) I become unconscious and, to a reasonable degree of medical certainty, I will not regain consciousness, or (3) the likely risks and burdens of treatment would outweigh the expected benefits, OR

(b) Choice To Prolong Life

I want my life to be prolonged as long as possible within the limits of generally accepted health care standards.

(2.2) RELIEF FROM PAIN: Except as I state in the following space, I direct that treatment for alleviation of pain or discomfort be provided at all times, even if it hastens my death:

_____

_____

(Add additional sheets if needed.)

(2.3) OTHER WISHES: (If you do not agree with any of the optional choices above and wish to write your own, or if you wish to add to the instructions you have given above, you may do so here.) I direct that:

_____

_____

(Add additional sheets if needed.)

PART 3
DONATION OF ORGANS AT DEATH (OPTIONAL)

(3.1) Upon my death (mark applicable box):
(a) I give any needed organs, tissues, or parts, OR
(b) I give the following organs, tissues, or parts only.

_____

(c) My gift is for the following purposes (strike any of the following you do not want):
    (1) Transplant
    (2) Therapy
    (3) Research
    (4) Education

PART 4
PRIMARY PHYSICIAN (OPTIONAL)
(4.1) I designate the following physician as my primary physician

_____

(name of physician)

_____

(address)   (city)   (state)   (ZIP Code)

_____

(phone)

OPTIONAL: If the physician I have designated above is not willing, able, or reasonably available to act as my primary physician, I designate the following physician as my primary physician:

_____

(name of physician)

_____

(address)   (city)   (state)   (ZIP Code)

_____

(phone)

PART 5

(5.1) EFFECT OF COPY: A copy of this form has the same effect as the original.

(5.2) SIGNATURE: Sign and date the form here:

_____

_____

(date)   (sign your name)

_____

(address)   (print your name)

_____

(city)   (state)

(5.3) STATEMENT OF WITNESSES: I declare under penalty of perjury under the laws of California (1) that the individual who signed or acknowledged this advance health care directive is personally known to me, or that the individual's identity was proven to me by convincing evidence (2) that the individual signed or acknowledged this advance directive in my presence, (3) that the individual appears to be of sound mind and under no duress, fraud, or undue influence, (4) that I am not a person appointed as agent by this advance directive, and (5) that I am not the individual's health care provider, an employee of the individual's health care provider, the operator of a community care facility, an employee of an operator of a of a community care facility, the operator of a residential care facility for the elderly, nor an employee of an operator of a residential care facility for the elderly.

First witness   Second witness

_____

_____
(print name)   (print name)

_____

_____
(address)   (address)

_____

_____
(city)   (state)   (city)   (state)

_____

_____
(signature of witness)   (signature of witness)

_____

_____
(date)   (date)

(5.4) ADDITIONAL STATEMENT OF WITNESSES: At
least one of the above witnesses must also sign the following
declaration:

I further declare under penalty of perjury under the laws
of California that I am not related to the individual executing this advance health care directive by blood, marriage,
or adoption, and to the best of my knowledge, I am not
entitled to any part of the individual's estate upon his or
her death under a will now existing or by operation or law.

_____
(signature of witness)   (signature of witness)

PART 6
SPECIAL WITNESS REQUIREMENT
(6.1) The following statement is required only if you are a
patient in a skilled nursing facility—a health care facility
that provides the following basic services: skilled nursing
care and supportive care to patients whose primary need is
for availability of skilled nursing care on an extended basis.
The patient advocate or ombudsman must sign the following
statement:

STATEMENT OF PATIENT ADVOCATE OR OMBUDSMAN

I declare under penalty of perjury under the laws of California that I am a patient advocate or ombudsman as designated by the State Department of Aging and that I am serving as a witness as required by Section 4675 of the Probate Code.

_____

(date)   (sign your name)

_____

(address)   (print your name)

_____

(city)   (state)

Rights of Next of Kin

As discussed previously, your next of kin has the right to make decisions for you if you do not create a health care directive. However, once you have executed a legally binding health care power of attorney, the choices you have made must be honored even if your next of kin does not agree with them. But because a lengthy court case can hold up the implementation of your wishes, it is a good idea to try to ensure cooperation of family in advance.

Storage and Access to Documents

Once you have executed a health care directive, you will want to give a copy to your physician, to the person you have named in your document as your proxy, and you will want to keep a copy at home. The original should be stored in a safe place, such as a small fireproof safe in your home. It should be readily accessible and not stored someplace such as a bank safe deposit box where access is only available during certain hours. Make sure that wherever you store it, it is protected from fire, flood, mold, dampness, and theft. The person you have named as your proxy should know where to find it in case of an emergency.

Anytime you check into the hospital, you should bring a copy of the document with you so that it will be on file should it need to be used, and there won't be any waiting period or confusion. Your attorney might suggest you actually sign several originals of this document so that all your doctors can have original binding documents.

You may also wish to register your document with the U.S. Living Will Registry (*www.uslivingwillregistry.com*). This free service will keep your directive in a safe place and make it accessible to health care providers at any time. This is particularly useful if you are someone who travels a lot or splits your time between two states.

Revocation

Once you execute a health care directive it stays in effect until you destroy it or execute a new health care directive. Destroying it might seem like a simple solution, but if you've given copies or additional originals to your doctors, getting them back can be difficult. Creating a new directive, or signing a legally binding document that says you revoke all prior health care directives, and then sending that document to all physicians, is the safest route.

Chapter 3

Pay Back:
Insurance and Financial Assistance

The cost of medical care continues to rise; it is a fact that if you want to obtain good health care in this country and are not independently wealthy, health insurance is essential. Fortunately though, there are many programs that make health insurance accessible now. If you are without insurance, there are still some options available to you.

Private Health Insurance

Health insurance is one of the most crucial types of insurance you can have because you use it on a regular basis and because medical care can be prohibitively expensive. But getting and maintaining health insurance is not as easy as it should be.

If you have a job that makes health insurance available, you should take it, even if you think you don't need it right now or think you can't afford the employee contributions. You can be denied insurance if you have a preexisting condition, however the Health Insurance Portability and Accountability Act (HIPAA) permits you to obtain coverage with a pre-existing condition if you previously had health insurance, but waiting periods may apply. The definition of a preexisting condition is a health condition for which you have received treatment for in the last six months and includes HIV. If you have a condition but do not receive treatment for six months, it can't be considered a preexisting condition.

Health Insurance Coverage for Partners

If you have a civil union or same-sex marriage and it is recognized by your state, your partner is able to obtain health insurance through you, and you through him or her. This is required for companies based in your state, but is also available from companies not based in your state. In Alaska, state employees with domestic partners are entitled to the same benefits of state employees with spouses. In addition, there are now many employers who make health insurance benefits available to domestic partners without any coercion by the state.

Additionally, some states and cities have equal benefits ordinances which require that any contractor that has a contract with the state or local government must offer the same benefits to domestic partners as to married spouses. The following states and cities require this:

- ✠ State of California (Effective January 2007. Until then San Francisco, Los Angeles, Berkeley, San Mateo County, and Oakland have laws in place.)

- Broward County, Florida has a preference for contractors that offers equal benefits.
- Miami Beach, Florida
- Minneapolis, Minnesota
- New York (A court recently struck down an equal benefits ordinance that New York City had in place.)
- Olympia, Seattle, Tumwater, and King County, Washington
- Salt Lake City, Utah has a preference for contractors that offers equal benefits.

If you are not legally entitled to health insurance and it is an added perk offered by your employer (something more and more employers are realizing they need to offer—in fact, the higher a company is on the Fortune 500 list, the more likely it is they will offer domestic partner benefits), you will most likely be required to provide an affidavit that states you are domestic partners. You may be asked to provide information about things such as financial support and whether your relationship is equivalent to a marriage. Some employers require proof of commingled finances such as joint bank accounts, mortgages, or leases. Check with your human resource department to find out what is required, or look in your employee manual.

Getting health insurance through a partner is an important benefit, and one that enhances the quality of life for so many couples, often permitting one partner to stay home and care for children or pursue a self-owned business. Unfortunately, these benefits continue to have detrimental legal and tax consequences for gay couples that do not apply to married couples. If you have to sign an affidavit about your living or financial situation together and any information you provide is false, the company could require you to repay the costs of the health insurance. This could also be grounds for termination of your job.

Domestic partner benefits also have important tax conse-quences. The IRS does not consider domestic partners, same-sex married couples, or civil union couples as married couples for the purposes of federal taxes. Because of this, the value of the health insurance received by the non-employed spouse is taxable income, unless he or she is legally a dependant of the employed spouse (someone who resides in his or her home and receives at least half of his or her support from that per-son). Employers are required to withhold and report taxes on these types of benefits. Also, additional fringe benefits extended to your partner (for example, free or reduced air-fare offered to spouses/partners of airline employees) would be considered taxable income. The value of these benefits are taxed to the employee, not the partner who is getting them. Taking advantage of these benefits results in an increase in taxable income, but without any actual increase in salary.

> To learn about employers that offer domestic partner benefits, visit *www.hrc.org/worknet*. There, you can download a manual about how to get these benefits to be offered through your employer.

COBRA

The Consolidated Omnibus Budget Reconciliation Act (COBRA) is a federal law that gives you the right to continue your health insurance after you leave a job. If you work at a company with 20 or more employees, you are eligible if you have one of the following qualifying events: you quit, are fired (except when you are fired for gross misconduct), or your hours are reduced (making you no longer eligible for employer provided health insurance). Under COBRA, you can continue your benefits (health insurance, prescription, vision, and dental plans) for up to 18 months if you take over paying the cost of the policy (in addition to a small administrative fee which can be charged). If you are disabled, you can continue the policy for up to 28 months. When you continue your COBRA coverage, you continue coverage for any dependents, such as partners or children as well. You have 30 days to decide if you want to elect coverage under COBRA after a qualifying event. When a heterosexual couple divorces, the spouse who is carried on the other's health insurance plan has the right to continue coverage under COBRA for 18 months. Because this is a federal law and the federal government defines marriage as only a man and a woman, COBRA rights are not extended to gay couples, even if they are married or have a civil union. There are some employers who recognize the inequity of this and voluntarily offer something similar to COBRA.

Flexible Spending Accounts

A Flexible Spending Account (FSA) is an account set up by your employer into which you can deposit money from your paycheck pre-tax, to pay for health care costs. These types of accounts are a great way to save money on taxes. At this time, you cannot use your FSA to pay for your partner's health care costs, even if he or she is carried on your employer-sponsored health insurance plan. There are no limits on how much you can contribute to an FSA, however most employers create a cap. The trick to FSAs, however, is that they are a "use it or lose it" proposition. You must use the money in the fund to pay for that year's medical expenses, or you forfeit the balance.

Because of this, you must carefully calculate what your expected expenses will be so that you do not put too much money in the account. Some FSAs now offer debit cards, which remove the hassle of having to save receipts and remit withdrawal forms.

Health Savings Accounts

Health Savings Accounts (HSAs) are special accounts that can only be used by those who have high deductible health insurance programs, sometimes also called catastrophic health care plans, because they only cover major illnesses. For 2006, the individual deductible must be at least $1,050 and $2,100 for a family plan. You place money in the account pre-tax and can invest it and let it grow. You use the funds to pay for your medical expenses. Unlike FSAs, these are not use-it-or-lose-it accounts and the amounts carry forward from year to year.

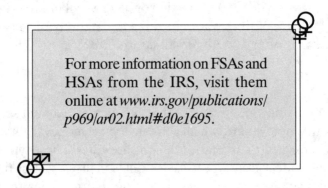

For more information on FSAs and HSAs from the IRS, visit them online at *www.irs.gov/publications/ p969/ar02.html#d0e1695*.

Health Insurance Coverage for Families

If you have health insurance available to you through your employer and you have children who are legally yours, you can put the children on your policy. If you and a partner have children together, but you are not the legal parent, you are not able to carry them on your policy. However, if you have coverage for domestic partners on your policy and get your partner on, then his or her legal children can also be covered.

Disability

If you have a private disability insurance policy, your employer has one, or if you live in one of the states with state disability insurance (New Jersey, New York, California, Hawaii, and Rhode Island), you are eligible for payments when you are temporarily disabled. Disability insurance usually pays approximately 60 percent of your salary.

Each policy is different, so it is important to carefully read your coverage. If you receive your coverage as a benefit of your employment, it is governed by a federal law called ERISA (Employment Retirement Income Security Act). Disability polices usually have two different levels of disability. The first is being unable to perform the duties of your job. Usually coverage is available under this standard for two to three years. The second level means you can't do any work at all, not just your own job.

Once you qualify for disability payments, maintaining your eligibility is key. This means working with your doctor to make sure your medical record accurately reflects your condition, including fatigue, sleeplessness, medication side effects, stamina, and all other symptoms, even if they become the norm for you. Your insurance company can request updates on your condition at any time.

If you are denied benefits, you must follow the appeals process laid out in your plan. For more information about private disability insurance plans and other problems you may face, visit *www.glad.org/rights/Disability_Benefits.pdf*.

If you become permanently disabled (AIDS—along with many other conditions—can lead to a permanent disability), you are eligible for SSDI (Social Security Disability Insurance). SSDI pays you a certain amount per month based on how much you have paid in FICA over the years. There is a five month waiting period from the time of disability until payments begin. If you have little income or have not worked for long, you may qualify for Supplemental Security Income. This program would include food stamps and Medicaid coverage. To apply, contact your local Social Security Administration office or go online to *www.ssa.gov*.

Read a fact sheet from the Social Security Administration called Social Security for People Living with HIV/AIDS at *www.ssa.gov/pubs/10019.pdf*.

Long-Term-Care Insurance

Long-term-care insurance is designed to pay some (usually not all) of a person's nursing home expenses, which can cost more than $70,000 per year. Long-term-care insurance is an important way to prevent the draining of personal and family finances and is available to all people. Long-term-care insurance is particularly of importance to the gay community because Medicaid spousal allowances, which sets aside some funds for a spouse's living expenses, are not available.

To become eligible for Medicaid, it is necessary to "spend down" so that your assets do not exceed Medicaid maximums. Gay partners don't have the same protections under Medicaid law and, if you own a home together, you could lose it if you need to spend down to Medicaid.

Purchasing long-term-care insurance avoids having to spend down, and offers you and your partner some financial stability. Instead of losing your assets to pay for medical care, you pay monthly premiums for a policy that will pay for long-term-care. The younger you are, and the better health you are in, the more sense purchasing such a policy makes, because the premiums will be lower. It is usually recommended that you consider a purchase like this in your 40s or 50s. For older people, it becomes a difficult question whether it is best to invest money or to pay a premium for insurance. If premiums are 5 percent or less of your income, then it is usually recommended that you purchase a policy.

Studies have shown that if a prior hospitalization is required for the policy to come into effect (you must first be hospitalized, then the policy will step up and pay for your long-term-care), there is a 50 percent chance you will never be able to collect any money from the policy.

Most policies are in effect as long as you pay your premiums and most contain a waiver for premiums while you are actually in long-term-care (so you aren't collecting on the policy and paying premiums at the same time).

When you consider a policy there are some considerations to take into account:

✚ Determine if the policy covers in-home care.

✚ Learn if the policy covers skilled, as well as unskilled, nursing home care.

✚ Find out if there is a waiting period before benefits can be paid.

✚ Check for inflation protection on policy limits.

✚ Examine all reimbursement levels and maximum benefits.

✚ Ask if premiums are set or fluctuating.

✚ Discuss the cancellation policy and be aware of who is responsible for it (either you or the insurance company).

✚ Make sure the policy is guaranteed to be renewable.

When considering long-term-care insurance, it is essential that you meet with a long-term-care insurance specialist who has worked with gay couples before. It is also important to choose an insurance company that is financially stable.

State and Federal Health Insurance

If you do not have a private insurance policy, there are other options available to you. Each state now offers insurance programs for children, and many also make these available to adults on a sliding scale. These policies are excellent options for uninsured singles or families. Check with your state health department or go online at *www.insurekidsnow.gov* to find out what is available to you.

In addition to state health insurance plans, there are a variety of free medical care options available to low-income families. Community health centers and public hospitals provide free care to those in need. Other programs include:

✚ **National Breast and Cervical Cancer Early Detection Program (NBCCEDP).** They provide free or low-cost mammograms and pap tests for women over the age of 39 who cannot afford breast exams or Pap smears. For more information, visit *www.cdc.gov/cancer/nbccedp/contacts.htm* or 1-888-842-6355.

⊕ **Maternal and Child Health Services**. State programs provide health care services for low-income women who are pregnant and their children under age 22. The federal government funds these programs and establishes general guidelines regarding services. Each state determines eligibility and identifies the specific services to be provided. For services available in your area, contact *https://performance.hrsa.gov/mchb/mchreports/link/state_links.asp*.

⊕ **Free clinics**. These clinics provide services for the working poor and uninsured. For a list of clinics in your area, contact *www.freeclinic.net* or call (540) 344-8242.

⊕ **Prescription drug assistance**. Some states provide prescription drug assistance to people who are not covered by Medicaid. Also, many drug companies will work with your doctor or health care provider to supply free medicines to those in need. For prescription drug resources, go to *www.disabilityresources.org/RX.html*.

⊕ **Women with cancer**. Women who are coping with cancer can find help through a variety of government-sponsored and volunteer organizations. Low-income and underserved women with breast and cervical cancers can obtain assistance online from *www.AvonBreastCare.org*.

⊕ **HIV**. The federal Ryan White CARE Act funds services for those with HIV/AIDS who are without insurance or financial resources to pay for care. For information call (888) 275-4772 or go to *http://hab.hrsa.gov*.

Many states also offer a high-risk pool for health insurance for those who cannot obtain coverage through other policies because they are excluded due to serious illnesses (such as HIV). For more information, visit *www.healthinsurance.org/riskpoolinfo.html*.

Medicare insurance is a federally-funded program that accrues benefits based on your earnings. You become eligible at age 65 and can apply three months before your birthday. If you are not eligible based on your earnings, you can purchase Medicare by paying premiums. To enroll, contact your local Social Security office. Medicare contracts with private health insurance companies to administer benefits, so even though you have Medicare, your health insurance card may say Blue Cross (or some other company) on it. Medicare coverage is limited and does not cover extended nursing home stays, glasses, hearing aids, physicals, private nurses, or dental care. There are two types of Medicare: Part A is hospital coverage and this is offered free if you qualify. Part B covers doctor visits, medical equipment, and prescriptions but there is a yearly fee to participate.

Medicaid is a federal program that is administered by the states, and provides health insurance for people who meet certain asset and income requirements. Many people spend down to become qualified for Medicaid, use up their assets, and then become eligible. There are certain items that are exempt from the Medicaid spend down. One of those rules permits a spouse to remain in the couple's home; however this rule does not apply to same-sex couples. Thus, there is a risk of the healthy spouse becoming homeless as part of the ill spouse's Medicaid eligibility spend down.

For more information, visit *www.Medicare.gov*.

Medigap Insurance

If you will soon be eligible for Medicare, you may wish to consider Medigap insurance. Medigap coverage is meant to bridge the gap between what Medicare does not cover and health care that is commonly needed. It is a good way to extend your coverage past Medicare minimums without the expense of purchasing an entire private health insurance policy. Medigap policies can cover Medicare premiums, co-pays, and deductibles. It is best to purchase this type of insurance within the first six months of Medicare coverage. There are 10 standard types of Medigap plans with varying levels of coverage. All include:

- ✚ 60–90 days of hospital stay with a lifetime reserve of 91–150 days.
- ✚ 365 days of hospital coverage after Medicare reimbursements.
- ✚ Part B physician coinsurance.
- ✚ Three pints of blood per year.

Additional coverage may include skilled nursing care, Part A and Part B deductibles, portions of bills not covered by Medicare, and preventive care.

Life Insurance

Life insurance is an important way to make sure your family will be provided for should something happen to you. The easiest way to get life insurance is if it is offered as a benefit of your employment. If not, you will need to apply for a purchase of an individual policy.

Unfortunately, naming your partner as beneficiary is difficult. The beneficiary is the person who is paid the face amount of the policy when the person insured dies a natural or accidental death. In order to be a beneficiary, the person you choose must have what is called an insurable interest in you. This means that he or she will suffer financial loss should you die. Common examples include spouses, children, and other family members. You would think it would be a no-brainer that a domestic partner would qualify, but many insurance companies still do not recognize that gay partners have an insurable interest in each other's lives.

If you encounter this kind of difficulty, you may need to show you are financially dependent on each other and own a home or share a lease together. But sometimes in those situations, insurance companies will limit the amount of the policy to the amount of the mortgage. If you are in a joint business venture together, this is yet another way to prove you have an insurable interest in each other. It is also possible to take out a policy and name a person with a clear insurable interest, such as a parent, and then later submit a form changing your beneficiary to your partner.

Life insurance can also be useful while you are alive, because you can use accelerated benefits to pay your benefits if you are terminally ill. (See Chapter 6 for more information.)

When you apply for life insurance, a medical exam, medical records, and blood work are required. Life insurance is available even if you have HIV. Premiums may be higher, but coverage does exist, even if you have to choose impaired risk life insurance. Impaired risk insurance is for those with limited life expectancies and the cost reflects that (in other words, it is higher). In most states, you can obtain guaranteed issue life insurance, regardless of your health, but again, the costs reflect the risk levels of the insurance. They also usually have a three year waiting period and do not pay if you die within the three year time frame.

If you already have life insurance and would like to increase the amount, ask about a guaranteed insurability rider. This clause gets added to your current policy and allows you to purchase additional insurance without going through a medical exam. Usually, when you seek to obtain or increase insurance, you must undergo a medical exam and your records in the Medical Information Bureau (see this online at *www.mib.com*) are searched. This databank shows if you have been tested for HIV (but not the result), as well as your medications. You can obtain one free copy of your file each year.

Remember that life insurance is not the best option for everyone. If you are single, it probably makes more sense to put your money into investments, with possibly a small burial policy if you wish. Additionally, there are other ways to ensure your partner has financial stability after your death, such as joint investments, or yearly tax-free gifts to your partner (up to $12,000 per year, but check current gift tax laws, as this number does change).

Charitable Remainder Trust

An alternative to life insurance is setting up a charitable remainder trust, which will provide you and your partner with a monthly income, and, after both of you die, the remainder of the trust will go to charity. This option only makes sense for couples who have a lot of financial means, because it essentially ties up large chunks of money and pays them back monthly—making the balance inaccessible.

Chapter 4

HIV

HIV is a part of life for many people. Learning what your rights are can help you access resources and become better informed. Until there is a cure, we'll always be striving for better care, more services, reduced discrimination, and increased funding. More than 80 percent of those with HIV are heterosexual. Although this is the case, it is still an important concern in the gay community.

Discrimination

Although there is no federal law prohibiting discrimination against gays and lesbians, there is a law prohibiting discrimination against people with HIV. The Americans with

Disabilities Act (ADA) prohibits discrimination against a person who has been diagnosed with HIV in the following situations:

✚ Employment: This includes hiring, firing, advancement, compensation, applicants, training, leave, layoff, tenure, and more. This provision applies to private (with at least 15 employees) and government employers.

✚ State and local government services.

✚ Public transportation.

✚ Public accommodations and services operated by public entities: This includes health care, hotels, stores, libraries, restaurants, and more. Private clubs and religious organizations are exempt.

✚ Telecommunications.

Employers cannot make any inquiry prior to employment about HIV and cannot require a medical exam. However, the employer can ask questions about a person's ability to perform certain tasks; a medical exam can be required after hiring if it is related to the job. Employers must make reasonable accommodations to the work place to allow employees to perform their duties, unless it imposes an undue hardship on the business. First an employee must ask for an accommodation.

An Ohio man recently successfully sued McDonald's for forcing him out of his job because he had HIV.

For employment specific concerns, contact the Equal Employment Opportunity Commission at *www.eeoc.gov* or call (800) 669-4000.

For public transportation concerns, contact:
Office of Civil Rights
Federal Transit Administration
U.S. Department of Transportation
400 Seventh Street, S.W. Room 9102
Washington, D.C. 20590
www.fta.dot.gov/ada
(888) 446-4511

For all other violations or for general information contact:
U.S. Department of Justice
Civil Rights Division
Disability Rights Section
P.O. Box 66738
Washington, D.C. 20035-6738
www.ada.gov
(800) 514-0301

In addition to the ADA, the federal Fair Housing Act provides protection for individuals with HIV. Under this act, real estate companies, landlords, mortgage bankers, homeowner insurance companies, and more cannot discriminate against individuals who are HIV positive. This means that someone cannot refuse to rent or sell to you because you have HIV, or refuse to offer you a mortgage. Additionally, under this act, a landlord must allow a tenant to make reasonable modifications to the property to accommodate his or her disability. To file a complaint, contact the Department of Housing and Urban Development using an online form available at *www.hud.gov/complaints/housediscrim.cfm* or by calling (800) 669-9777. You can reach them by mail at:

Office of Program Compliance and Disability Rights
Office of Fair Housing and Equal Opportunity
U.S. Department of Housing and Urban Development
451 7th Street, S.W. Room 5242
Washington, D.C. 20410

HIV Testing

HIV testing is one of the most important things *any* adult (gay or straight) can do to protect his or her health. However, it is absolutely your right to decide if you wish to be tested. Though no one can force you to be tested, there are many employers who try to compel applicants to do so. Under the Americans with Disabilities Act (ADA) you cannot be asked about medical conditions when you are applying for a job.

You cannot be discriminated against because of your HIV status and an employer cannot ask about your status or what medication you take during the hiring process. Any testing done after you are hired must be done for all employees and HIV status cannot be used to fire or demote you. Currently it is not illegal for a health care provider to refuse to treat you because of your HIV status, though there are some state and local laws that prohibit this kind of discrimination.

You cannot be denied housing or credit because of your HIV status. You cannot be denied the right to adopt a child or to spend time with your own child because you are HIV positive.

It should also be noted that patients are sometimes tested for HIV without their knowledge during medical care such as pregnancy and when surgery is scheduled. In New York, HIV screening is mandatory during pregnancy, but in other instances, this type of testing violates informed consent. The Center for Disease Control (CDC) also recommends that all pregnant women be tested for HIV.

Free tests for HIV are available at federal, state, and local health departments, as well as Planned Parenthood clinics. Some offer tests that are completely anonymous, while other tests are "confidential," which means your name is used, but it protected. In Idaho, Iowa, Mississippi, Nevada, North Carolina, North Dakota, South Carolina, South Dakota, and Tennessee, the state does not permit anonymous tests. All states require that HIV test results be reported to the state department of health for statistical purposes. In total, 38 states require that names be reported, but there are privacy protections in place to protect that information from dissemination (although having your name on any list like this would seem to be a violation of privacy). The following states use code-based reporting, where each person is assigned a code and is identified only by code:

- ✚ California
- ✚ Hawaii
- ✚ Illinois
- ✚ Maryland
- ✚ Massachusetts
- ✚ Rhode Island
- ✚ Vermont
- ✚ Washington
- ✚ Washington, D.C.

The following states use what is called name-to-code based reporting, where names are initially reported but then are assigned codes:

- ✚ Delaware
- ✚ Maine
- ✚ Montana

✚ Oregon has just changed over to a system where records are kept by name. If you have questions about your state laws, call your state health department.

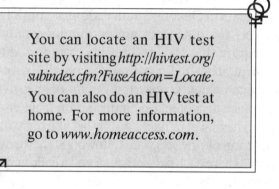

You can locate an HIV test site by visiting *http://hivtest.org/subindex.cfm?FuseAction=Locate*. You can also do an HIV test at home. For more information, go to *www.homeaccess.com*.

HIV Partner Notification Laws

HIV status is an intensely private matter, however there is a public health component that has led to partner notification laws. If someone has been exposed to HIV through sexual activity or needle sharing, that is important information for him or her to know. The problem comes in when you try to balance privacy with the right to know. Both people involved have equally compelling interests and choosing how to balance them is not always easy. Partner notification is not always a cut and dry issue—notifying a former or current partner could result in violence, discrimination, and other severe repercussions against the person who could have transmitted the virus.

Today the Center for Disease Control (CDC) mandates that all states have HIV partner counseling and referral services (PCRS). These are systems in which current or past partners of people with positive HIV tests can be notified by the state, with the consent of the patient. Notification of partners is purely voluntary (if you don't want to provide notification, you don't have to) in all states at this point, however, Delaware, New Jersey, and Washington, D.C. have laws that permit notification against a patient's will if a court order is obtained.

One important thing to remember about partner notification, should it ever become mandatory, is that partners can only be notified if the person being tested provides the partner's name. So in a sense, partner notification will always be voluntary.

There is also a federal law that requires HIV infected persons to notify their spouses, which under federal law refers to heterosexual marriages. Note that this law probably does not apply in Massachusetts because Massachusetts same-sex marriage is not recognized by the federal government; this law could apply to GLBT persons who are legally married to a person of the opposite sex.

There are no laws that require health care providers to disclose their HIV status to patients. There is no need for this because all health care workers should use universal precautions (gloves, masks, and so on) to prevent HIV transmission from provider to patient and from patient to provider. There has never been a proven case of HIV transmission from health care provider to patient. There is also no requirement that a patient disclose his or her HIV status to a health care provider because universal precautions provide protection.

Liability for HIV Transmission

All states have generic criminal laws that could be used to prosecute people who knowingly expose others to HIV through sexual conduct, and the following states have specific public health laws that prohibit exposure of STDs (sexually transmitted diseases, also called sexually transmitted infections, or STIs):

- ✚ Alabama
- ✚ California
- ✚ Colorado
- ✚ Florida
- ✚ Idaho
- ✚ Kansas
- ✚ Kentucky
- ✚ Louisiana
- ✚ Maryland
- ✚ Montana
- ✚ Nevada
- ✚ New Jersey
- ✚ New York
- ✚ North Dakota
- ✚ Oklahoma
- ✚ Oregon
- ✚ Rhode Island
- ✚ South Carolina
- ✚ South Dakota
- ✚ Tennessee
- ✚ Utah
- ✚ Vermont
- ✚ Washington
- ✚ Wyoming

In a recent Georgia case, a man pled guilty to reckless conduct and was sentenced to two years in jail for having unprotected sex with a partner and not informing him he was HIV positive.

It's important to remember that knowingly exposing another to HIV, in addition to being a criminal offense, could made you civilly liable as well—for pain and suffering as well as medical costs.

Denial of Benefits

If you have HIV, you cannot be denied health insurance under the Americans with Disabilities Act simply because of this. If your employer has 15 or more employees and offers health insurance, you cannot be denied coverage, unless the plan has a policy that excludes those with serious illnesses. There have been some lawsuits against insurance companies who place caps on coverage for HIV, but the Supreme Court has declined to hear them.

If health insurance is offered as an "open enrollment," you will not be asked about your health conditions and you will not be required to take any blood tests. If this is not the case though, then you can be asked to consent to a blood test and to disclose your health conditions. If you have a prescription plan, you cannot be denied coverage for medically necessary drugs, such as azidothymidine (AZT).

If you have health insurance and a claim is denied, you must follow the appeals process laid out in your plan. When seeking an appeal, it is essential that your physician agree with you that coverage should be provided, because the determination will be made based on the medical records.

Preventive HIV Medications

Unfortunately there is no vaccine or clear preventive treatment for HIV. However, one drug, Tenofovir, which is used as a treatment for HIV, has been shown to have anti-HIV preventive properties. There are some physicians who will prescribe this drug for patients who engage in behavior that warrants it. It is also sometimes prescribed for partners of those who have HIV. Some strains of HIV are resistant to this drug, so it is by no means a sure thing. The drug has possible side effects, so it is not for everyone. It is available as an oral medication and also as a gel.

As a patient, it is your right to ask your physician about this drug and other possibilities. You can't force a physician to prescribe something for you, so if you're not happy with the response you get, you can see another physician. The problem you are likely to encounter is that the drug has not been approved by the FDA for this use, so a prescription for it would be an off-label use, which puts the physician more at risk if there is a problem with it. You're likely to get the best results if you go into the conversation armed with knowledge, so do some online searches about this drug and its possibilities first.

HIV and Health Insurance

The Ryan White CARE Act provides health care for individuals with HIV who have financial need. The act provides funding from the federal government to pay for health care, testing, prevention, hospice care, case management, and more. Many states have HIV Insurance Continuation Assistance Programs (ICAPs) which pay for insurance for those who are unable to continue working and cannot pay for health insurance. Check with your state department of health for information about this kind of program. Your premiums cannot be higher because you have HIV.

If you have HIV, you may also be eligible for reimbursed dental care under the federal Dental Reimbursement Program. This program reimburses dental school clinics for care they provide to HIV patients.

The American Academy of HIV Medicine is an organization of physicians who specialize in the care and treatment of HIV. Contact them at *www.aahivm.org* or (202) 659-0699.

AIDS Drugs Assistance

Each state has a program that offers assistance affording drugs for HIV/AIDS to underinsured and uninsured people. To qualify, you must not exceed maximum income levels that differ by state. Some states also offer free HIV/AIDS health care at specific clinics.

For more information, see *www.thebody.com/financial/adap.html*. In addition to the state programs, drug companies also offer patient assistance programs. Each company has its own enrollment program, but generally you will be required to show proof of income, citizenship, prescription, and insurance denial. For more information, see *www.atdn.org/access/states*.

To find more information on HIV treatment, funding, and assistance, go online to *www.aidsinfo.nih.gov*.

HIV and Travel Insurance

For travel insurance, HIV is considered a preexisting condition if it is not stable for 60 days prior to the purchase of the policy. Changes in medication, change in symptoms, or progression of the illness can be enough for a denial. Many travel insurance policies no longer include preexisting condition exclusions though, so when purchasing a policy, be sure to inquire about this. It is also important to note that most travel insurance policies do not define spouse to mean same-sex partner, so it may be necessary to purchase separate policies.

HIV Housing Assistance

About 65 percent of people with HIV/AIDS report that after medical care, housing is their biggest need. In addition to this, 1/3 to 1/2 of all people with AIDS are homeless or in danger of losing their homes. A federal law, Housing Opportunities for People With AIDS (HOPWA) was passed in 1990. Funding goes directly to communities so that they can fund housing alternatives for those in need.

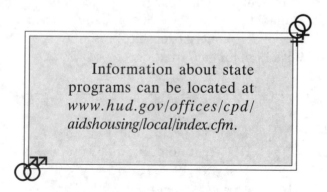

Information about state programs can be located at *www.hud.gov/offices/cpd/ aidshousing/local/index.cfm.*

Marijuana for Medical Use

Medical marijuana is a treatment for AIDS wasting because it relieves nausea and vomiting and can offer pain relief. Alaska, California, Colorado, Hawaii, Maine, Maryland, Nevada, Oregon, Vermont and Washington have made medical use of marijuana legal (when prescribed by a doctor), but the problem is that federal laws criminalizing marijuana supercede state laws, meaning even if it is legal in your state, you can still be prosecuted under the federal law. The issue made it to the Supreme Court in the case *United States v. Oakland Cannabis Buyer's Club*, but the ruling does not invalidate the state laws. State and local law enforcement cannot prosecute users of medical marijuana in those states, but federal officials can.

Chapter 5

Dollars and Sense:
Finances and Documents

Unfortunately, money is a big part of health care and health care decisions. Even if you have health insurance, there are still a multitude of financial issues that impact, or are impacted by your health. Taking steps to make sure your financial security is protected should you or your partner become ill can offer great peace of mind.

Powers of Attorney

A power of attorney is an essential document that every gay man or lesbian should have. A power of attorney is a legal document that authorizes another person to handle your financial, business, or personal affairs (such as banking, bill paying, real estate, and so on) for you. If you have a partner, this type of document is going to be one of your key protections. A significant fact you need to understand about a power of attorney document, however, is that the person you select will be able to do anything he or she wants with your bank accounts, investments, real estate, and so on, so it's essential that you select someone whom you trust completely. The person acting on your behalf does not have to consult you or act in a way he or she thinks you would have acted had you been able.

There are several types of powers of attorney to choose from. A durable power of attorney becomes active at the moment you sign it, allowing your partner, or whoever you have chosen, to begin handling your affairs immediately. Note though that just because it's legal doesn't mean it has to be used. You and your partner (or whomever else you select) may have a clear understanding about when you will step in to manage each other's affairs. The important thing about this type of power of attorney is that it's ready to go at a moment's notice. This type of document can also be useful in your daily life when illness is not a factor, allowing you to do financial or real estate transactions on each other's behalf. If you're in a domestic partnership, this is a document you should have no matter what, even if you aren't experiencing any health problems.

A springing power of attorney is another type that goes into effect upon the happening of a future event specified in the document, such as becoming incapacitated. This type of document works well if you're naming someone who is not your partner to step in should you become ill—only in a "what if" scenario. The person you select has no powers or authority until the happening of the specified event. This is a good choice if you're naming a friend or relative and not a partner.

It is important to see an attorney in your state so that you can obtain an acceptable power of attorney because each state has its own form set out by statute. If you have bank accounts and want to specifically name a person who can handle those for you, your bank can provide the form you need to complete. These forms will govern only the accounts at that bank. It is possible to purchase power of attorney forms at legal stationery stores, paralegal services, or self-help Websites, but you must know how to complete them in order for them to be effective. They need to be notarized, but this is something you can have done at your bank for no fee.

Once you have executed a power of attorney, it is a good idea to keep it in a safe place and make sure that the person you have named is aware of where it is. It is not recommended that you hand over the form to the person you have selected unless it is your partner. Also, you should not keep it in a bank safe deposit box because the only one who can access your personal safe deposit box is you, and if you're incapacitated, no one is going to be able to access the document. It is important to talk to the person you name in the document and make sure he or she is willing to accept this responsibility. You don't want it to be a surprise and you don't want him or her to refuse to handle things at the 11th hour.

Note that power of attorney forms do not deal with health care decisions and also do not give the authority to make decisions for one's children (such as medical decisions or education decisions).

The following is a sample power of attorney:

DURABLE GENERAL POWER OF ATTORNEY
NEW YORK STATUTORY SHORT FORM

THE POWERS YOU GRANT BELOW CONTINUE TO BE EFFECTIVE SHOULD YOU BECOME DISABLED OR INCOMPETENT (CAUTION: THIS IS AN IMPORTANT DOCUMENT. IT GIVES THE PERSON WHOM YOU DESIGNATE (YOUR "AGENT") BROAD POWERS TO HANDLE YOUR PROPERTY DURING YOUR LIFETIME, WHICH MAY INCLUDE POWERS TO MORTGAGE, SELL, OR OTHERWISE DISPOSE OF ANY REAL OR PERSONAL PROPERTY WITHOUT ADVANCE NOTICE TO YOU OR APPROVAL BY YOU. THESE POWERS WILL CONTINUE TO EXIST EVEN AFTER YOU BECOME DISABLED OR INCOMPETENT. THESE POWERS ARE EXPLAINED MORE FULLY IN NEW YORK GENERAL OBLIGATIONS LAW, ARTICLE 5, TITLE 15, SECTIONS 5-1502A THROUGH 5-1503, WHICH EXPRESSLY PERMIT THE USE OF ANY OTHER OR DIFFERENT FORM OF POWER OF ATTORNEY. THIS DOCUMENT DOES NOT AUTHORIZE ANYONE TO MAKE MEDICAL OR OTHER HEALTH CARE DECISIONS. YOU MAY EXECUTE A HEALTH CARE PROXY TO DO THIS. IF THERE IS ANYTHING ABOUT THIS FORM THAT YOU DO NOT UNDERSTAND, YOU SHOULD ASK A LAWYER TO EXPLAIN IT TO YOU.)

THIS is intended to constitute a DURABLE GENERAL POWER OF ATTORNEY pursuant to Article 5, Title 15 of the New York General Obligations Law:

I,_____

(insert your name and address)

do hereby appoint:

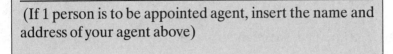

(If 1 person is to be appointed agent, insert the name and address of your agent above)

_____

_____

_____

_____

(If 2 or more persons are to be appointed agents by you insert their names and addresses above)

my attorney(s)-in-fact TO ACT (If more than one agent is designated, CHOOSE ONE of the following two choices by putting your initials in ONE of the blank spaces to the left of your choice:)

( ) Each agent may SEPARATELY act.

( ) All agents must act TOGETHER.

(If neither blank space is initialed, the agents will be required to act TOGETHER) IN MY NAME, PLACE AND STEAD in any way which I myself could do, if I were personally present, with respect to the following matters as each of them is defined in Title 15 of Article 5 of the New York General Obligations Law to the extent that I am permitted by law to act through an agent:

(DIRECTIONS: Initial in the blank space to the left of your choice any one or more of the following lettered subdivisions as to which you WANT to give your agent authority. If the blank space to the left of any particular lettered subdivision is NOT initialed, NO AUTHORITY WILL BE GRANTED for matters that are included in that subdivision. Alternatively, the letter corresponding to each power you wish to grant may be written or typed on the blank line in subdivision "(Q)", and you may then put your initials in the blank space to the left of subdivision "(Q)" in order to grant each of the powers so indicated).

( ) (A) real estate transactions;

( ) (B) chattel and goods transactions;

( ) (C) bond, share and commodity transactions;

( ) (D) banking transactions;

( ) (E) business operating transactions;

( ) (F) insurance transactions;

( ) (G) estate transactions;

( ) (H) claims and litigation;

( ) (I) personal relationships and affairs;

( ) (J) benefits from military service;

( ) (K) records, reports and statements;

( ) (L) retirement benefit transactions;

( )(M) making gifts to my spouse, children and more remote descendants, and parents, not to exceed in the aggregate $10,000 to each of such persons in any year;

( ) (N) tax matters;

( ) (O) all other matters;

( ) (P) full and unqualified authority to my attorney(s)-in-fact to delegate any or all of the foregoing powers to any person or persons whom my attorney(s)-in-fact shall select;

( ) (Q) each of the above matters identified by the following letters:

_____

(Special provisions and limitations may be included in the statutory short form durable power of attorney only if they conform to the requirements of section 5-1503 of the New York General Obligations Law.)

_____

_____

_____

This durable Power of Attorney shall not be affected by my subsequent disability or incompetence.

If every agent named above is unable or unwilling to serve, I appoint

_____

(insert name and address of successor) to be my agent for all purposes hereunder.

TO INDUCE ANY THIRD PARTY TO ACT HERE-UNDER, I HEREBY AGREE THAT ANY THIRD PARTY RECEIVING A DULY EXECUTED COPY OR FAC-SIMILE OF THIS INSTRUMENT MAY ACT HEREUN-DER, AND THAT REVOCATION OR TERMINATION HEREOF SHALL BE INEFFECTIVE AS TO SUCH THIRD PARTY UNLESS AND UNTIL ACTUAL NO-TICE OR KNOWLEDGE OF SUCH REVOCATION OR TERMINATION SHALL HAVE BEEN RECEIVED BY SUCH THIRD PARTY, AND I FOR MYSELF AND FOR MY HEIRS, EXECUTORS, LEGAL REPRESENTA-TIVES AND ASSIGNS, HEREBY AGREE TO INDEM-NIFY AND HOLD HARMLESS ANY SUCH THIRD PARTY FROM AND AGAINST ANY AND ALL CLAIMS THAT MAY ARISE AGAINST SUCH THIRD PARTY BY REASON OF SUCH THIRD PARTY HAVING RELIED ON THE PROVISIONS OF THIS INSTRUMENT. THIS DURABLE GENERAL POWER OF ATTORNEY MAY BE REVOKED BY ME AT ANY TIME.

In Witness Whereof I have hereunto signed my name this _____ day of_____, 19____

_____

(Signature of Principal) (You sign here)

Responsibility for Medical Bills

Medical bills can be a very worrisome thing, particularly if you become seriously ill or do not have health insurance. Your health must be your number-one priority, with concerns about money coming in a distant second. Many people worry that their partners will end up paying off their bills. There are only certain situations in which your bills can impact your partner.

If you and your partner own joint assets, you could be required to sell the asset so that your ownership portion can be used to pay the bills. If, for example, we are talking about a house, your partner could buy your ownership portion from you, giving you cash to use for medical bills. There are some situations in which your partner is required to use his or her assets to pay your bills. The first would be if you are married or in a civil union, or in a California domestic partnership; many of your assets would be considered joint. Additionally, New Jersey domestic partnership law makes partners mutually responsible for each other's support, so it is possible that as the partner of a patient, you could be required to pay medical costs.

The thing to remember about medical bills is that there is a lot of assistance available for them so, sometimes, a hospital social worker may be able to recommend programs that might provide financial assistance. When thinking about all of your other regular household bills, you do have some options for those during illness as well. Many creditors are willing to place your bill in deferment while you are ill—with no payments due and no negative impact to your credit. The best thing you can do is ask and plead your case. If HIV is the reason for your disability, be sure to mention that because HIV patients are able to receive more benefits.

People often wonder what happens to medical bills for a person who is deceased. They worry that their partner or family members will be required to pay the bills. The bills are applied against the deceased person's estate. If there is not enough in the estate, the person's partner, family, or children are not responsible for the bills.

Credit and HIV

If you have been diagnosed with HIV, it is a good idea to start thinking now about ways to improve your credit report. You may get to a point where you need a lot of credit and if you work now to pay down your debts and improve your credit ratings, you will benefit from it later. And of course, keeping good credit is important for everyone, regardless of health. If don't have a good handle on your current debt situation, you should request your credit reports. There are three major credit reporting agencies: Trans Union, Equifax, and Experian. A credit report is similar to a financial report card. It lists all of your debts, loans, credit cards, foreclosures, bankruptcies, liens, and judgments. The credit report and the credit score (a number assigned to each person after a quick measurement of how good their credit it) are the first things that potential new creditors look at. Credit reports are also accessed by potential employers and potential landlords, so they can have far-reaching effects.

You can now obtain one free credit report from each of the three credit reporting agencies each year. You can download it online at *www.annualcreditreport.com* or call to request it at 1-877-322-8228. When you get your credit report, read it carefully and check for errors—accounts you paid off, accounts which are not overdue but are reported as overdue, incorrect account numbers, and so on. If you find any errors, report them immediately to the company that prepared your report.

Once you have your credit report, you can begin to work on paying down outstanding balances, reaching payment plans with creditors (they are open to them), and closing accounts you no longer use. If you find yourself in a situation where you're in over your head, anyone can submit a 100 word statement to the credit reporting agencies. This statement can be used to explain extenuating circumstances, such as illness, losing a job, and so on. The statement will appear on your credit report for future potential creditors to consider.

Consumer credit counseling is an option that will help you consolidate your bills into one monthly payment, which can make things easier. Credit counseling services also often teach budgeting and money management techniques that can be useful. To locate a credit counseling agency, or for more information, contact the National Foundation for Credit Counseling at *www.nfcc.org* or (800) 388-2227.

Another added protection to consider if you have HIV and are trying to put some safeguards in place is to purchase insurance for your credit cards, so that should you be unable to pay the bills, the insurance will do so for you.

Flexible Spending Accounts

Flexible spending accounts (FSAs) are an important way to save on medical costs. If your employer offers an FSA, you put some money aside pre-tax (directly out of your paycheck—the money is not counted towards your taxable income) into a special account. You can then use this money to pay health care costs that are not covered by your insurance, such as co-pays, deductibles, prescriptions, dental care, vision care, and more. Because these accounts are a federal tax tool, same-sex married couples, civil union couples, and domestic partners cannot use them to pay for a partner's costs—only for your own. Flexible spending accounts are discussed in greater depth in Chapter 3.

Wills

A will is an essential part of your complete health care and future plans. Wills are of particular importance for the gay community because of the inequities in which gay couples are treated under the laws in many states. If you do not have a will, your assets and belongings will be divided according to your state's intestacy law. If you die without a will, your assets will be given to:

⊕ Legal spouses (Same-sex marriages and civil union couples fit this category, as well domestic partners in California and Maine, and reciprocal beneficiaries in Hawaii)

⊕ Legal children

⊕ Parents

⊕ Siblings

If you have a partner, have no will, and are not legally joined in the eyes of your state, he or she is entitled to nothing if you die. In New Jersey, a law was recently passed giving a surviving partner control of the estate and inheritance. If you and your partner have children together, but you are not a legal parent, your children cannot automatically inherit from you. If you have adopted children, they are considered to be legal children and are not treated any differently than biological children.

A will gives you the choice of how your assets and belongings will be distributed after your death. You can leave anything you want to anyone you want in your will. You have the option of leaving certain items or amounts to certain people, or the entire thing to one person, as well as leaving money or assets to charities. Note that a will has no impact on life insurance. To change a life insurance beneficiary, you must complete a beneficiary change form from your insurance company.

If you are legally married in your state your spouse has what is called the *right of election*. He or she can apply to get a portion of your estate simply because you are married, regardless of what the will says. This law is in place to make sure that spouses can't write each out of their wills, and is intended as a spousal support protection.

It is important to have a will professionally drawn up. Not only are there state requirements for how it must be written, executed, and witnessed, but it is also important to gain an understanding of estate tax law, so that you can maximize your assets. Assets that you pass through your will to a partner are taxed—they do not qualify for the federal marital deduction.

Once you have a will, discuss with your attorney where it will be kept. Some attorneys recommend you file it for safe-keeping at the local probate court, where it is kept in a vault. Other attorneys will keep it for you. Still, others might recommend you place it in a fireproof box or safe place at home. Once you have a will, there are two ways to change it or invalidate it. You can rip up the originals of the will and throw them out. You can also execute an amendment or codicil to the will which changes or adds to what was in the original will. The original will is upheld, but with the changes that you make to it. A codicil or amendment to the will must be executed properly to be effective, so be sure to talk to your attorney if this is something you are considering.

Estate Tax

The estate tax is a tax charged on taxable assets that are passed at your death. Congress is rolling back the estate tax through 2010, but there are no guarantees about what will happen after that date. In 2006, only estates worth more than $2 million have to pay estate tax.

Generation-Skipping Tax

The generation-skipping tax is one that many people are not familiar with. The tax applies when a bequest is made in a will to someone who is more than one generation away—such as a grandchild, grandniece, or grandnephew. The gift is considered to have skipped a generation (and skipped being assessed estate tax for that generation). This makes up for the tax the government is missing out on by applying a flat 55-percent tax on anything over the current gift tax exemption. This tax is also being phased out through 2010, but is yet to be determined if it will be reinstated at that point or not.

Gifts During Life

You can give up to $12,000 per person (under current law) per year during your life (with a lifetime total of $1 million) without triggering the gift tax. This is an important way to share assets with a partner or children. It's important to note that cash gifts are difficult to trace, but gifts given by check or transfer of securities are easier to trace.

Trusts are another way to give money or property during life. A trust allows you to transfer ownership but maintain control over the asset. The money or asset is placed in a legal trust and the income from it is paid to the beneficiary (the person you choose). A living trust gives you complete control over the assets, and the power to terminate the trust at any time you wish. The income is paid to the beneficiary and ownership passes to him or her upon your death. The advantage of a living trust is that it allows you to completely bypass probate, the court process of validating a will, and there is no way to contest a trust.

If you own a home together, it is likely that you own it as joint tenants with right of survivorship, which means that if one of you dies, the home goes to the other partner. This is an important way to pass assets, however, what you must understand is that, upon your death, what is considered to have been your ownership portion is going to be taxed as part of your estate, unless your partner can prove he or she financially contributed to that half.

If you have a large net worth, it is essential to see an estate planning attorney who can help maximize your assets and protect your dependents. You can find an attorney who specializes in this by contacting your local bar association or the National Council of Trust and Estate Attorneys at *www.actec.org*.

Living Trust

A living trust is a type of estate planning where you place all or some of your property/assets in a trust. You name a trustee who will manage the property/assets. You can then continue to use the assets and property in the trust during your lifetime. Once you die, the remainder of the trust passes to the person or persons you have chosen as beneficiaries. The items in the trust do not go through probate and are not subject to estate tax. Most living trusts are revocable, which means you can change your mind about them. If you're considering a living trust, it is important to talk to an experienced state planning attorney, who is skilled in Medicaid planning.

To learn more about living trusts, read this information sheet provided by the . Federal Trade Commission on online at *www.ftc.gov/bcp/conline/pubs/services/livtrust.htm*.

Retirement Plans

If you have money in a retirement account, it is important that you list your partner as the beneficiary on the account. Even if you don't think you are able to list your partner as a beneficiary it pays to check, because, for example, couples in New York State who married in Canada are treated as spouses under the state retirement system. It's also important to note that should you die first, your partner will be taxed on those benefits, unlike married heterosexual couples, because he or she will not be permitted to rollover the funds into his or her own account. Gay couples are not permitted to collect Social Security survivor benefits, so in planning for retirement it is essential to note that a partner's Social Security benefits die along with him or her, and will not continue to be paid to the surviving partner, although benefits will be paid to minor legal children.

Chapter 6

The White Coats:
Hospitals and Doctors

Many people tend to feel a bit helpless or intimidated when dealing with health care professionals, and especially with hospitals. Often it seems there is a system in place that moves things along without regard to personal wishes, needs, or feelings. It can all feel very impersonal and money-oriented. Not only is there existing prejudice with which to contend, but there are legal roadblocks that make it difficult to have your wishes respected.

The important thing to remember when dealing with the medical bureaucracy is that health care providers, hospital, clinics, and so on, are there to provide you with a service.

They are not in charge of your body or your treatment—you are. There are procedures that you need to work around or with, but the bottom line is that you have the absolute right to say what will happen to your body and all decisions that are made must be yours. They work for you, and although the system isn't always set up to respect that, it is a fact. Keep this in mind in all your dealings with medical personnel—it helps you put things into perspective. Your job is to find the right way to communicate your needs and wishes to your health care providers—which means understanding the laws and what your options are. When you are an educated health care consumer, you can make the best choices.

Does Your Health Care Provider Need to Know You Are Gay?

There are different answers to this question depending on your situation, and what kind of health care provider with whom you are dealing. For example, there is probably no reason your dentist would need to know you are gay or lesbian. That fact does not change the type of care you would need or receive. The bottom line is that you are never *required* to tell anyone you are gay, but there are some instances where providing that information can mean receiving health care that is better suited for you and your needs.

When dealing with family doctors, internists, OB/GYNs, or general practitioners who provide your primary health care, it may make sense to discuss the fact that you are gay, lesbian, bi or trans, if you believe this could have an impact on your health. For example, hepatitis vaccines are a good idea for sexually active gay men, as well as HIV tests. In most medical situations, your sexual life is not going to be important. There is some research that suggests lesbians are at a higher risk for breast cancer because many never give birth or breastfeed, so this may be something worth discussing with your health care provider.

There are some health care providers who will infer you are gay or lesbian, and that's not a problem as long as it does not change the manner in which you are treated. In fact, it can help if it means there is a higher level of understanding between the two of you. Your goal should be to find a gay-friendly health care provider who will treat you with respect and professionalism. If you need assistance, the Gay and Lesbian Medical Association (*www.glma.org*) has a searchable provider database on their Website. Don't be afraid to call in advance and ask if a doctor is gay-friendly before you make an appointment.

HIV Status

You are not required to tell any health care provider if you have HIV. You don't need to worry about safety, because all health care professionals use universal precautions for all patients and disclosure would not change the way they do anything. The only time disclosure might be important is if an accidental exposure happens—such as a health care provider getting an accidental stick with a needle used on a patient. In that situation, you would be asked to provide your status.

HIV status can be important in terms of your care though, so it is important to disclose it, and any medications you are taking, to physicians who will be providing care for you, as well as information about your current status. You want to receive knowledgeable care and in order for this to happen, your doctor needs to know your complete medical history.

Important Issues to Discuss With Your Health Care Provider

As the patient, it is often up to you to ask the right questions and discuss concerns for your health. As a gay man or lesbian, you are at a higher risk for a variety of health conditions, of which you may not be aware. Here are a few of the important issues you should discuss with your health care provider if you are concerned about their impact on your life:

Men:

- ✚ **STDs:** Gay men are at a higher risk.
- ✚ **Cancer rates:** Gay men are at a higher risk for prostate, testicular, and colon cancers.
- ✚ **Hepatitis immunization:** Gay men are at a higher risk for contracting this.
- ✚ **Alcohol/drug use:** Gay men have higher rates of substance abuse than other men.
- ✚ **Depression/anxiety:** Gay men are more likely to be depressed than other men.

Women:

- ✚ **Obesity:** Many lesbians have a higher body mass than other women, and obesity raises risk factors for heart disease, diabetes, and cancer.
- ✚ **Nutrition:** Studies show that lesbians are less likely to eat a healthy diet than other women.

- ✚ **Increased smoking:** Lesbians have higher levels of tobacco use than other women.

- ✚ **Depression/anxiety:** Lesbians have higher rates of depression than other women.

- ✚ **Alcohol/drug use:** Lesbians have higher substance-abuse rates than other women.

- ✚ **Cancer:** Endometrial, breast, and ovarian are important cancers to discuss with your provider because women who do not give birth and breastfeed are at higher risk.

- ✚ **Domestic violence:** Lesbians are at a lower risk than other women, but are more likely to stay silent if they are in danger.

- ✚ **Polycystic Ovarian Syndrome (PCOS):** This metabolic and hormonal syndrome affects 10 percent of all women and is often undiagnosed in women who are not concerned about ovulation, and is also common in women who are overweight.

- ✚ **STDs:** Lesbians are at risk of contracting the same STDs as other women, yet awareness of this is not very high among health care providers or lesbians themselves.

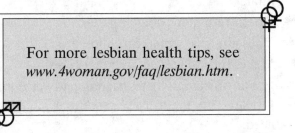

For more lesbian health tips, see *www.4woman.gov/faq/lesbian.htm*.

Finding Gay-Friendly Health Care Providers

You have the absolute right to select a health care provider who meets all of your criteria and is someone you feel comfortable with and can trust. Finding a gay-friendly provider is much easier than it used to be. The Gay and Lesbian Medical Association (*www.glma.org*) can provide online referrals to providers in your area. You may also be able to locate providers by word of mouth, through friends, or your local pride organization. You may also wish to check the ads for local gay events for providers who advertise.

If you're unable to get a solid recommendation for someone in your area, you'll need to take other steps. If you have a gay-friendly family doctor, for instance, and need to find a gay-friendly endocrinologist, ask him or her for a referral.

If you've been referred to a health care provider but aren't sure if he or she is gay-friendly, you can call and ask. If you still aren't sure, schedule a consultation and find out for yourself based on how he or she treats you. You want a health care provider who:

✚ Looks you directly in the eye without hesitation.

✚ Smiles and is friendly.

✚ Doesn't stumble over gay issues.

✚ Does not treat you like a child.

✚ Makes time to answer your questions.

✚ Has an office staff that is friendly and welcoming.

✚ Provides the kind of care and experience you need.

✚ Accepts your insurance.

✚ Is nonjudgmental.
✚ Treats your health care similar to a partnership, with you as an equal partner.

Defining Family

Hospitals confer many rights on family, but this is usually interpreted to mean heterosexual spouses, parents, siblings, and so on, and to exclude partners. You will be interested to know that the Joint Commission on Accreditation of Healthcare Organizations (JCAHO), an organization that accredits hospitals, defines family as, "The person(s) who plays a significant role in the individual's [patient's] life. This may include a person(s) not legally related to the individual" (Joint Commission Resources JCR, *2001 Hospital Accreditation Standards*, p. 322).

Although JCAHO defines family in this way, hospitals themselves do not necessarily follow this recommendation, and because of this, it is important to protect yourselves in an as many ways as possible.

Hospital Visitation Rights

When a person is hospitalized, visitation can be limited to close relatives only. There are many instances where this is not the case—hospitals are not usually frisking people at the doors and asking for ID and a family tree. However, if the next of kin (parents, siblings, and so on) wish to restrict access to a very ill patient, they can do so if that patient is unable to speak for him- or herself. Additionally when a patient is in an Intensive Care Unit, visitors may be restricted.

If you have a partner, it is very important that you take steps to allow him or her to visit should you ever become hospitalized and unable to express your wishes. Even if you believe that right now your family would not deny your partner visitation, it's a good idea to completely protect yourselves in case something should change in the future. The best way to ensure your partner will have access to you is to complete a written authorization and have it notarized. You can write or type up this authorization yourself:

Hospital Visitation Authorization

I _____ (name), residing at _____ (address) make this authorization of my own free will. In the event I am hospitalized in any hospital, medical facility, nursing home, rehabilitative care center, or any other medical care institution, I authorize my partner _____ (partner's name) to have first priority to visit me and spend time with me. This authorization is made in addition to/in place of (choose one) authorization made by any other persons who are related to me. I reserve the right to give different instructions once I am able to communicate.

_____

Name   Signature   Date

Notary:

You may wish to execute several originals of this document. Give one to your partner. Keep another at home with your health care directive document so that you can take both with you should you make a planned visit to the hospital. You may also wish to give an original to your primary care physician for his or her records.

Should you ever wish to change this document, you can either destroy all the originals or execute a new one and specify, "I hereby revoke any earlier hospital authorizations executed by me, and substitute this document."

In certain states, partners have hospital visitation rights by law, but it is a very good idea to execute an authorization anyhow in case you are hospitalized in a different state or the laws in your state change. Couples are granted hospital visitation rights by law in the following states:

- ✚ **Connecticut:** Civil union couples
- ✚ **California:** Domestic partners
- ✚ **Hawaii:** Reciprocal beneficiaries
- ✚ **Massachusetts:** Married couples
- ✚ **New Jersey:** Domestic partners
- ✚ **New York:** Domestic partners
- ✚ **Vermont:** Civil union couples

Note that the right to visit someone in the hospital does not automatically include the right to talk to his or her doctors and get updates. Use a health care directive (Chapter 2) to give your partner this important right.

Emergency Contact Cards

Should you be taken ill suddenly or injured in an accident and taken to a hospital, the hospital or emergency personnel will rely on you and your personal effects to provide contact information for your spouse or next of kin. If you are unable to communicate, the emergency personnel will check your purse, wallet, car, or bag for information. If you don't have an emergency contact card, they will try to locate a relative by contacting your physician (if they know who it is) and asking who is listed in your file, calling your residence as listed on your license, or seeking contact information for a relative in the phone book or directory.

To control who is contacted, it is a good idea to create an emergency contact card and carry it in your wallet or bag. You can cut an index card down to the size of a credit card, or just use a piece of paper. It's a good idea to get this laminated, which you can do at an office supply store. You can also now purchase wallet size pre-cut laminated plastic sleeves at Walmart which will fit right over the card.

Emergency Contact Information

In case of emergency, contact:

Name: _____

Relationship: _____

Home Phone: _____

Cell Phone: _____

Pager: _____

Address: _____

It is also a good idea to list any allergies, your blood type and the contact information for your primary care physician. If you have any medical issues such as diabetes, it is also wise to list these. If you take any medications on a regular basis, list that information, too.

Medical Decisions in a Hospital Setting

Hospitals have procedures for how health care decisions should be made for patients who are unable to make their own decisions. The next of kin is given priority in making decisions. If you have a health care directive (see Chapter 2) and a hospital visitation authorization, you have covered as many bases as you can to give your partner access and decision-making authority. What you and your partner need to know is that while these documents give you legal authority to essentially act as each other's next of kin, there may be situations in which you have difficulty getting a doctor or department in a hospital to recognize your authority. If someone refuses to recognize your authority, don't let them stop you. You should first ask to speak to the department head, then the administration. All hospitals also have patient advocates whose role is to assist patients and families with any concerns or problems that come up. Call the switchboard and ask to speak to one and explain your situation. Every hospital has a board and, if need be, you can always take your concerns there. Make it clear that you know your rights and intend to exercise them. If you have documentation, such as a health care directive giving you authority, and you cannot get the hospital to honor it, you need to contact an attorney who specializes in health care law. Call your local bar association for a referral.

Unfortunately, there have been many cases in which partners have been denied access to their partners or not allowed to exercise their authority to make decisions. In a Maryland case, *Flanigan v. A Maryland Hospital*, a partner was not permitted to see or speak to his dying partner or make decisions even though he was authorized to in a health care directive. The surviving partner sued, but the jury found for the hospital because a partner did not fall into the definition of family as the hospital defined it.

The American Medical Association House of Delegates passed a resolution supporting the recognition of partners for hospital visitation in 2001. However this is just a resolution, not a policy, and each hospital makes its own policies.

If you are unable to get access to your partner or make decisions for him or her and the hospital will not budge, you can call JCAHO and file a complaint, asking them to investigate the situation. Call them at (800) 994-6610 or e-mail at *complaint@jcaho.org*.

Visiting Hours

Most hospitals have specific visiting hours, to which visitors are asked to adhere, which are normally held in the late morning and afternoon hours. However, if you have a loved one in ICU, there may be different, shorter hours or there may be longer open hours during which you may only visit for very brief periods of time. No matter what the set visiting hours are for the area of the hospital your loved one is in, the attending physician can always give permission for you to stay longer, particularly in situations where the patient is terminal or critical. Situations can also arise where a patient cannot be calmed down and the nursing staff asks you to be there outside of visiting hours. The nursing staff may be understanding (the key of course is to make sure they like you) and allow bending of the rules at other times.

There are times when you might feel you can't, or don't, want to leave a partner or loved one alone in a hospital overnight. Many hospital rooms have chairs that fold out into cots. Visitors are not permitted in hospital beds, except in rare circumstances. If they won't let you stay in the room, you may be able to stay in a waiting room close by and ask the nursing staff to come get you if something changes.

If you're not able to stay overnight, but are extremely concerned about the type of care your partner or loved one is receiving, it is possible to hire private duty nurses who care only for one patient. This is an expense not covered by insurance and can be quite costly. To find a nurse, ask the nursing staff, or call an area nurse's association for a referral. The hospital patient advocate or social worker may also be able to provide a referral.

The American Hospital Association has created a brochure called The Patient Care Partnership, which can be viewed at *www.aha.org/aha/ptcommunication/partnership/index.html*. This is a revision of what used to be called the Patient's Bill of Rights and is designed to clearly explain a patient's rights and responsibilities in a hospital setting.

HIPAA Privacy

The Health Insurance Portability and Accountability Act (HIPAA) provided sweeping changes to health care privacy rights. Under this privacy act, health care providers cannot share medical information with any person without your permission. If you want your partner, or anyone else, to be able to have any access to your medical records (which might include calling your doctor with a question for you or on his or her own), you will need to execute a form giving specific permission for this. When you go to your doctor's office, be sure to ask for the authorization form. This is something you want to authorize in advance, and not have to worry about in the middle of a health care crisis. They will keep it in your file and you won't have to worry about it.

Under HIPAA, you have the right to access your own medical records, although a "reasonable" fee can be charged for copying. These fees vary by state. (For more information see *www.lamblawoffice.com/medical-records-copying-charges.html* for a list of state statutory maximum medical record copying fees). You also have the right to make additions to your records yourself (an important right if you disagree with a diagnosis, or believe information has been left out of your record). If you are in the hospital, you must give permission for your name and condition to be listed in the hospital directory (so that people can call your room, locate your room, receive deliveries, or call to find out about your condition).

Chapter 7

Terminal Illness

Terminal illness is something that is difficult to face, whether it is affecting you, or a partner. When dealing with terminal illness, there are a lot of issues to consider, in addition to the emotional pain. Making educated decisions will help everyone have some control through this painful time. Working with a physician whom you trust is an important step in the process.

Coping With Bad News

When you first get bad news, it can be difficult to deal with for everyone involved. The most important thing is to get a grip on the medical facts. If you need a second opinion, get one.

Contact your insurance company to determine what you need to do to make sure it is covered. Look into alternative treatments and therapies, and research everything online so that you are knowledgeable and able to ask the right questions.

The next step is coping with the emotions of the situation. This may be a good time to seek help from a therapist, grief counselor, clergy member, or other trained professional. Whether you are the ill person or the partner, this is a time when you have no choice but to focus on the important things first and worry about other things later. This is the time when you must prioritize without feeling guilty about it.

Organ Transplants

If you or a partner is in need of an organ transplant, you need to be aware of some problems that have cropped up in this area. You would not expect that a person could be denied an organ transplant simply because he or she is gay. Unfortunately, there have been incidents where this has occurred. There is no CDC policy that prohibits the transfer of donor organs to a gay male or female. Candidates are supposed to be individually evaluated for suitability and then placed on the list in order of need. HIV status is considered in evaluating a patient's prognosis. It's important to note that a 2002 study in the *New England Journal of Medicine* said that organ transplants in HIV positive patients should not be considered experimental and that survival rates among HIV positive patients who are receiving retro-viral treatments are not any different than those in other patients.

Some health insurance plans (notably Medicaid) have refused to cover the cost of organ transplants to HIV positive patients. However, the tide seems to be turning with the doctors involved, and most transplant centers know that HIV alone is not a reason to deny a transplant patient life-saving treatment. There have been several cases in which HIV positive people have been denied transplants by insurance companies, even though their HIV prognosis is good. Lambda Legal has successfully worked on behalf of several patients and persuaded insurance companies to cover the cost of transplants for them.

Should an insurance denial happen to you or a partner, it is imperative that you immediately begin the appeals process through your insurance company and then contact Lambda Legal (*www.lambdalegal.org*) or another reliable legal source for assistance.

California has a law that says insurers cannot deny a transplant based on a patient's HIV status. In 2005, an administrative law judge in Phoenix held that an HIV positive woman could not be denied a transplant because of her HIV status.

DNRs

DNR stands for "do not resuscitate" and it is entered into your hospital medical record so medical personnel know how to treat you. This means that you have chosen not to accept CPR to restart your heart or breathing. Many terminally ill people choose this because they do not wish to prolong their lives. If you or a partner chooses a DNR, you will need to discuss it with the primary physician and sign a hospital form indicating this wish. A DNR can be revoked at any time, either by the person who executed it, or by the person chosen to have health care power of attorney.

Document Check

Once you've gotten to a point where you've been able to make medical decisions and find a way to start to emotionally dealing with the situation, it is important to do a document check. Make sure that you or your partner have and can easily find:

- ✚ A valid, current will.
- ✚ A health care directive.
- ✚ Powers of attorney.
- ✚ A DNR if you wish.
- ✚ Hospital visitation authorization.

Some people also wish to get their financial records in order. This is something that is a matter of personal choice, so only do what feels right to you. If you wish to do so, you may want to gather:

- ✚ Life insurance policies (including small polices provided by credit card companies and employers).
- ✚ Retirement and pension plan records.
- ✚ Banking and investment account information.
- ✚ Deeds to real estate.
- ✚ Titles for vehicles.
- ✚ A list of all credit cards and your regular monthly bills.
- ✚ Homeowners and auto insurance information.
- ✚ Information about safe deposit boxes.
- ✚ Combinations or keys for safes you have at home.
- ✚ Passwords for e-mail and internet accounts.

Viatical Settlements and Living Benefits

Life insurance can be of use to you or your partner during life and does not have to be something that is saved as a death benefit for survivors. Living benefits or accelerated benefits allow a policy holder to collect money from the policy in order to pay for long-term care, health care, or simply for living expenses during a terminal illness. Taking this kind of benefit is, in essence, an early payment of the policy's death benefit. If you use up the entire accelerated benefits allotment, there will be no death benefit remaining upon your death. If your policy does not have a living benefits clause, it may be possible add a rider to the policy giving you this option. If this is an option you are considering, talk with your financial planner to first to determine if it makes sense. You need to examine all of your assets and create a financial plan that takes into consideration your needs and your family's need. Contact your insurance agent for information on how take a living benefit if that is what you decide to do.

Another option is a viatical settlement. A viatical settlement occurs when you sell your death benefit to a company that specializes in this kind of transaction. The company purchases your policy for a portion (often 60 to 90 percent) of the face value (the amount payable at death). When you die, the policy is then payable to that company. They make a profit when they get the full death benefit after paying only a portion of its value. In order to qualify for a viatical settlement you must:

- ✚ Be terminally ill.
- ✚ Allow the purchasing company to have access to your medical records to prove your life expectancy.
- ✚ Have owned the policy for at least two years.
- ✚ Get your beneficiary to agree to the sale. (Note: You can change your beneficiary first if you think you might encounter opposition.)

A viatical settlement can be a financial relief for those whose financial resources are dwindling due to terminal illness; the downside is you end up leaving nothing to your beneficiary. If life insurance was part of your financial support plan for your partner or family, this can be a difficult decision to make. Many people plan to rely on life insurance policies to cover funeral costs, and if a viatical settlement is used, funeral costs will have to come out of your estate, or be paid by loved ones.

Finding a viatical settlement when you have HIV has become more difficult simply because the life expectancy for those with this disease has increased so drastically (a wonderful thing, but something that makes turning a profit very difficult for these companies).

Choosing a reputable company for a viatical settlement is essential. Evaluate possible companies in this way:

1. First, get several offers from several companies so that you have a good comparison.
2. Contact your state attorney general's office and ask if there are any complaints against any of the companies you are considering.
3. Ask if the company you are dealing with is self-funded or a broker. If they are brokers, ask what their commission is (this comes off the money you would get otherwise).
4. Go over the contract with your attorney and tax planner before agreeing to anything.
5. Request that all funds for the purchase be placed in escrow so they can be verified and secured and will be easily accessible after the sale.
6. Make sure that payment will be made upon signing.

The more seriously ill you are, the larger the sum of money you can expect to negotiate (because the company will receive the death benefit sooner). The money you receive from this is taxable income.

Some people have found that creating their own viatical settlement makes more sense. Name a relative as your beneficiary, then borrow money from him or her (including interest, so it is not taxed). Payment is made as payment of your death benefit. Additionally there are other options available when you need cash. You could:

- ✚ Sell your home.
- ✚ Sell other property.
- ✚ Sell investments.
- ✚ Research other health care options (such as Medicaid).
- ✚ Ask older relatives if you could receive any possible inheritance now instead of receiving it upon their death.

Reverse Mortgages

A reverse mortgage allows a homeowner to continue living in his or her own home, while mortgaging it to a company that pays a monthly payment or gives a lump sum payment while the owner continues to live in the home. In this sort of arrangement, what you're doing is selling the equity in your home to the company in exchange for cash. This solution is attractive for those who reach a point where they cannot afford to stay in their homes. The end result is that, when you die, your home has little if any cash value left in it. Obviously, if your partner or family plans to continue to live in the home, this option is not a good one. But if you are single and own your own home, this can be a way to get cash and make your life comfortable.

A reverse mortgage can be a better choice than a home equity loan because foreclosure is not an option. With a home equity loan, at some point, you will be required to make payments to pay back the loan. With a reverse mortgage that is never the case.

The Federal Housing Authority insures some reverse mortgages, but only for homeowners who are more than 62 years of age and who own the home free and clear, or with a low mortgage balance.

Funeral Decisions

Many people wish to make decisions about their own funerals, and whether you are considering your funeral in light of a terminal illness, or simply in the light of making plans for the inevitable, you have rights with respect to your funeral.

You can prepay for a funeral through a funeral home and make all the arrangements, down to the smallest details. Making this kind of arrangement ensures you will have the send-off that you choose. However, you should note that while you can control the disposition of your body, you can't stop a family member or other person from holding a separate memorial service or church service in your honor after you have passed.

If you do prepay for funeral services be sure to:

✚ Keep the paperwork in a place where your partner or family knows to look. Do not use a safe deposit box because it could be sealed upon your death.

✚ Specify to whom any overpayment you made should be refunded to.

- ✚ Verify that your purchase includes services as well as products (such as a casket).
- ✚ Ask if the plan is transferable if you move.

You can also specify your wishes about funerals in your will, but the problem with this is that wills are not usually probated until long after the funeral and it would not be enforceable.

In the past, there were some funeral homes that refused to handle arrangements for those who died of AIDS or HIV. Fortunately, this is no longer a common situation at all. If you should encounter such a situation, contact Lambda Legal or an attorney.

Burial and Cremation

You have the right to specify how you want your body handled and disposed of after your death. You can choose the site of burial, decide if you want to be embalmed, or select cremation as an option. If you foresee that there will be two separate memorial services, you can specify that you be cremated and your remains divided between the two groups. To specify your wishes, include them in your will or in a separate notarized document and make sure your family and loved ones know where to locate these documents and know in advance what your wishes are.

You can prepay for a burial plot or a place for your ashes to rest. You can also specify whether your ashes should be scattered or kept by a loved one. (Note that there are legal restrictionsregarding where ashes can be scattered.)

New York State recently passed a law that allows residents to specify a person whom they wish to handle the disposition of their body. Under the law, a simple document similar to a health care proxy can be completed. If no document is completed, the law creates a descending list of next of kin who would have decision-making authority. Domestic partners are included in this law on par with heterosexual spouses.

Hospice Care

Hospice or palliative care is in-home or residential care for patients with life-ending illnesses. Hospice care follows a carefully constructed model that focuses on supporting both the patient, family, and loved ones, while managing pain and providing a comfortable end of life. The emphasis is on dignified death that is as pain-free as possible, not on treating the actual illness (because when you turn to hospice care you have already tried every other option). Hospice care is not designed to either shorten or extend life, but to make the end to life a good experience. Hospice care usually does not involve feeding tubes, life support systems, or aggressive treatment. The goal is to manage pain while helping the patient be as cognizant as possible. The approach that is taken is holistic and encompasses every aspect of the patient's life.

To qualify for hospice care, your physician must certify that you have a life expectancy of six months or less. In order for hospice care to be covered by insurance, your physician must make the referral to hospice care. Hospice programs are very proactive and initiate contact immediately once they receive a referral.

The hospice approach is team-based. A family member or loved one becomes the team leader and works with physicians, nurses, aides, therapists, dieticians, social workers, counselors, and other health care workers. The emphasis is on providing care for the entire family unit; bereavement counseling continues for at least one year after the end of life. An important program through a hospice is respite care, when other team members provide care, allowing loved ones much needed time alone or time off. When caring for a terminally ill family member, you must make time to care for yourself.

When selecting a hospice program, first confirm insurance coverage. If you have several programs to choose from, get some information and ask questions such as:

- How long they have been in service?
- What is their approach and philosophy?
- Do they offer home-based or residential treatment?
- Are they gay-friendly and able to work with gay partners?
- What services do they provide for children?
- What professionals are on each team?
- Besides pain management, what other services do they offer?
- What kind of grief counseling do they offer?
- What documentation do they need?
- How many patients do they serve at one time?
- Are there 24-hour services and assistance available?
- Can you talk to some families that have used their service?

For more information about hospice care, contact the National Hospice and Palliative Care Organization at (800) 658-8898 or *www.nhpco.org*.

Assisted Suicide

Assisted suicide is a criminal act in 44 states. North Carolina, Utah, and Wyoming have no laws about assisted suicide and Ohio has a court ruling which says it is not a crime to assist in a suicide. Virginia has no criminal laws, but does have civil laws which impose sanctions on those who assist suicides.

Oregon permits very specific physician-assisted suicide under the Death With Dignity Act—physicians can prescribe pills for the patient to take on his or her own; however, no other kind of assistance is legal. In Oregon, there is no official process under the law for determining when a patient qualifies for assisted suicide, but instead, this is left up to individual physicians and their patients to make these decisions together as long as the patient:

- ✚ Is 18 years of age or older.
- ✚ Is a resident of the state of Oregon.
- ✚ Is capable of making and communicating health care decisions for himself.
- ✚ Has been diagnosed with a terminal illness that will lead to death within six months.

It's up to the physician to establish that the patient has met the criteria set out by the state's laws.

The following steps must be followed:

1. The patient must make two oral requests for assistance, at least 15 days apart, to the physician. The physician can offer the patient the opportunity to withdraw the request (and the patient can withdraw it any time on his own).
2. The patient then must provide a written request to the physician, which must be signed by two

witnesses, at least one of whom is not a relative of the patient.

3. The physician and a consulting physician must confirm the diagnosis.

4. The physician and consulting physician must determine if the patient can make medical decisions for himself.

5. If either physician believes the patient's judgment is impaired by a psychiatric or psychological disorder, the patient must be referred for a psychological examination.

6. The physician must inform the patient of alternatives to assisted suicide including comfort care, hospice care, and pain control.

7. The physician must ask the patient to inform next of kin of the decision and the plan, but cannot require that this be done.

There is nothing that says a person cannot move to Oregon and establish residency in order to make use of the law. The patient must be a current resident of the state and it is up to the physician to determine that this is the case. Note that the law allows M.D.s (medical doctors) as well as D.O.s (doctors of osteopathy), to assist suicides. Under Oregon law, this type of assisted suicide is not legally considered suicide and thus health insurance companies will pay the costs involved, but you need to check your policy for specific restrictions.

Following is a sample form that must be used in Oregon to begin the process for physician assisted suicide.

REQUEST FOR MEDICATION
TO END MY LIFE IN A HUMANE AND DIGNIFIED MANNER

I, _____, am an adult of sound mind.
       First   Middle   Last

I am suffering from _____, which my attending/prescribing physician has
determined is a terminal disease and which has been medically confirmed by a consulting physician.

I have been fully informed of: my diagnosis; prognosis; the nature of medication to be prescribed and potential
associated risks; the expected result; and feasible alternatives, including comfort care, hospice care and pain control.

I request that my attending/prescribing physician prescribe medication that will end my life in a humane and dignified
manner and also contact any pharmacist to fill the prescription.

Initial One

[____]   I have informed my family of my decision and taken their opinions into consideration.

[____]   I have decided not to inform my family of my decision.

[____]   I have no family to inform of my decision.

I understand that I have the right to rescind this request at any time.

I understand the full import of this request and I expect to die when I take the medication to be prescribed.

I make this request voluntarily and without reservation, and I accept full moral responsibility for my actions.

I further understand that although most deaths occur within three hours, my death may take longer and my physician
has counseled me about this possibility.

Signature:	County of Residence:	Date:

DECLARATION OF WITNESSES

By *initialing* and *signing* below, we declare that the person making and signing the above request:

Witness 1   Witness 2

[____]   [____]   1. Is personally known to us or has provided proof of identity;

[____]   [____]   2. **Signed this request in our presence on the date following the person's signature;**

[____]   [____]   3. Appears to be of sound mind and not under duress, fraud or undue influence;

[____]   [____]   4. Is not a patient for whom either of us is the attending physician.

Printed Name:	Signature:	Date:
Witness 1		
Printed Name:	Signature:	Date:
Witness 2		

NOTE: One witness shall not be a relative (by blood, marriage or adoption) of the person signing this request,
shall not be entitled to any portion of the person's estate upon death and shall not own, operate or be employed
at a health care facility where the person is a patient or resident. If the patient is an inpatient at a long-term
health care facility, one of the witnesses shall be an individual designated by the facility.

Copies of this form are available at http://egov.oregon.gov/DHS/ph/pas/index.shtml.   Rev. 04/06

For more information on Oregon's Death With Dignity Act, see *http://egov.oregon.gov/DHS/ph/pas/faqs.shtml*.

When considering assisted suicide, in addition to the primary concern of relieving suffering in a gentle way, it is important to make sure that anyone involved in the process will not be prosecuted, which means you need to be aware of the laws in your state and how your arrangement will be handled by the authorities.

Life insurance policies typically will not pay death benefits for assisted suicide (or any other kind of suicide) if it occurs within one or two years of the date the policy is taken out. If you have a life insurance policy and are considering assisted suicide, it is very important that you check the policy carefully for this exclusion.

For more information on euthanasia, assisted suicide, suicide, and physician-assisted suicide, visit *www.finalexit.org*.

Chapter 8

Time Off:
Leave for Yourself
or Your Partner

Illness or injury is something that takes time and care to recuperate from. If you become ill or injured, taking time off from work to recover can be a crucial part of your recovery. If you have a partner who is ill or injured and needs to be cared for, being able to take time off without loss of job security can be an incredible benefit.

Federal Family and Medical Leave Act Law

The federal Family and Medical Leave Act (FMLA) is an important piece of legislation that allows workers to take time off from work to recover from an illness or to care for a close family member who is ill. FMLA can be used to take time off for your own illness, to care for a family member, or to care for a new child in the family. Unfortunately, the federal law does not include a same-sex partner in its definition of close family members (because the federal Defense of Marriage Act (DOMA) defines marriage as between a man and a woman), but there are many employers who will treat your partner as a close family member and offer you similar benefits. See later in this chapter for more information.

To qualify for federal FMLA leave for your own medical condition, you must work for an employer with at least 50 employees who work within 75 miles of each other. So, if you work for an employer that has 25 employees in California and 25 in New York, they aren't covered. You must have been employed there at least 12 months (these do not have to be consecutive months) and worked at least 1,250 hours. You can take up to a total of 12 weeks of leave in a 12 month period. You can take all the leave at once or spread the leave out so that you work some or all of the time on a part-time basis. When possible, you must give 30 days notice of the leave (in emergency situations, no notice is required). When you return to work, your employer must reinstate you to your job or to a similar position. All FMLA leave is unpaid. Note that you are entitled to no more than 12 weeks of leave in each 12 month period, whether you use that leave for your own illness or to care for a child or family member, or for both.

If you are a key employee—a salaried employee who is among the highest paid 10 percent of employees within 75 miles of the work site—the employer can refuse to reinstate you to the same position upon your return if it will cause severe economic injury to the company's operations. In order for this exception to apply though, you must have maintained your health insurance during your FMLA leave. The employer must notify you when he or she determines you will not be reinstated, and give you the opportunity to return to the same position then if you wish.

When you take a leave for your own health reasons, the law requires that your medical condition be a "serious health condition" and that you have:

- ✛ A period of time requiring hospital or residential care.

- ✛ A period of incapacity that requires two or more visits to health care providers or medical personnel, or one visit that results in subsequent continuing treatment.

- ✛ Incapacity due to a chronic serious health condition that requires periodic health care visits, continues over a period of time, and can cause episodes of incapacity.

You will be required to provide certification from a doctor about your serious health condition. Following on the next four pages is the form you must have your physician complete to certify your medical condition. You can locate a copy online at *www.dol.gov/esa/regs/compliance/whd/fmla/wh380.pdf*.

Certification of Health Care Provider
(Family and Medical Leave Act of 1993)

U.S. Department of Labor
Employment Standards Administration
Wage and Hour Division

*(When completed, this form goes to the employee, **Not to the Department of Labor**.)*	OMB No.: 1215-0181 Expires: 08-31-2007

1. Employee's Name	2. Patient's Name *(If different from employee)*

3. Page 4 describes what is meant by a **"serious health condition"** under the Family and Medical Leave Act. Does the patient's condition[1] qualify under any of the categories described? If so, please check the applicable category.

   (1) _____ (2) _____ (3) _____ (4) _____ (5) _____ (6) _____ , or None of the above _____

4. Describe the **medical facts** which support your certification, including a brief statement as to how the medical facts meet the criteria of one of these categories:

5. a. State the approximate **date** the condition commenced, and the probable duration of the condition (and also the probable duration of the patient's present **incapacity**[2] if different):

   b. Will it be necessary for the employee to take work only **intermittently or to work on a less than full schedule** as a result of the condition (including for treatment described in Item 6 below)?

   If yes, give the probable duration:

   c. If the condition is a **chronic condition** (condition #4) or **pregnancy**, state whether the patient is presently incapacitated[2] and the likely duration and frequency of **episodes of incapacity**[2]:

---

[1] Here and elsewhere on this form, the information sought relates **only** to the condition for which the employee is taking FMLA leave.

[2] "Incapacity," for purposes of FMLA, is defined to mean inability to work, attend school or perform other regular daily activities due to the serious health condition, treatment therefor, or recovery therefrom.

Form WH-380
Revised December 1999

6. a. If additional **treatments** will be required for the condition, provide an estimate of the probable number of such treatments.

   If the patient will be absent from work or other daily activities because of **treatment** on an **intermittent** or **part-time** basis, also provide an estimate of the probable number of and interval between such treatments, actual or estimated dates of treatment if known, and period required for recovery if any:

   b. If any of these treatments will be provided by **another provider of health services** (e.g., physical therapist), please state the nature of the treatments:

   c. **If a regimen of continuing treatment** by the patient is required under your supervision, provide a general description of such regimen (*e.g.*, prescription drugs, physical therapy requiring special equipment):

7. a. If medical leave is required for the employee's **absence from work** because of the **employee's own condition** (including absences due to pregnancy or a chronic condition), is the employee **unable to perform work** of any kind?

   b. If able to perform some work, is the employee **unable to perform any one or more of the essential functions of the employee's job** (the employee or the employer should supply you with information about the essential job functions)? If yes, please list the essential functions the employee is unable to perform:

   c. If neither a. nor b. applies, is it necessary for the employee to be **absent from work for treatment**?

8. a. If leave is required to **care for a family member** of the employee with a serious health condition, **does the patient require assistance** for basic medical or personal needs or safety, or for transportation?

   b. If no, would the employee's presence to provide **psychological comfort** be beneficial to the patient or assist in the patient's recovery?

   c. If the patient will need care only **intermittently** or on a part-time basis, please indicate the probable **duration** of this need:

Signature of Health Care Provider

Type of Practice

Address

Telephone Number

Date

To be completed by the employee needing family leave to care for a family member:

State the care you will provide and an estimate of the period during which care will be provided, including a schedule if leave is to be taken intermittently or if it will be necessary for you to work less than a full schedule:

Employee Signature

Date

A **"Serious Health Condition"** means an illness, injury impairment, or physical or mental condition that involves one of the following:

1. Hospital Care

   Inpatient care (*i.e.*, an overnight stay) in a hospital, hospice, or residential medical care facility, including any period of incapacity[2] or subsequent treatment in connection with or consequent to such inpatient care.

2. Absence Plus Treatment

   (a) A period of incapacity[2] of **more than three consecutive calendar days** (including any subsequent treatment or period of incapacity[2] relating to the same condition), that also involves:

   (1) **Treatment[3] two or more times** by a health care provider, by a nurse or physician's assistant under direct supervision of a health care provider, or by a provider of health care services (*e.g.*, physical therapist) under orders of, or on referral by, a health care provider; or

   (2) **Treatment** by a health care provider on **at least one occasion** which results in a **regimen of continuing treatment[4]** under the supervision of the health care provider.

3. Pregnancy

   Any period of incapacity due to **pregnancy**, or for **prenatal care**.

4. Chronic Conditions Requiring Treatments

   A **chronic condition** which:

   (1) Requires **periodic visits** for treatment by a health care provider, or by a nurse or physician's assistant under direct supervision of a health care provider;

   (2) Continues over an **extended period of time** (including recurring episodes of a single underlying condition); and

   (3) May cause **episodic** rather than a continuing period of incapacity[2] (*e.g.*, asthma, diabetes, epilepsy, etc.).

5. Permanent/Long-term Conditions Requiring Supervision

   A period of **Incapacity[2]** which is **permanent or long-term** due to a condition for which treatment may not be effective. The employee or family member must be **under the continuing supervision of, but need not be receiving active treatment by, a health care provider**. Examples include Alzheimer's, a severe stroke, or the terminal stages of a disease.

6. Multiple Treatments (Non-Chronic Conditions)

   Any period of absence to receive **multiple treatments** (including any period of recovery therefrom) by a health care provider or by a provider of health care services under orders of, or on referral by, a health care provider, either for **restorative surgery** after an accident or other injury, **or** for a condition that **would likely result in a period of Incapacity[2] of more than three consecutive calendar days in the absence of medical intervention or treatment**, such as cancer (chemotherapy, radiation, etc.), severe arthritis (physical therapy), and kidney disease (dialysis).

This optional form may be used by employees to satisfy a mandatory requirement to furnish a medical certification (when requested) from a health care provider, including second or third opinions and recertification (29 CFR 825.306).

Note: Persons are not required to respond to this collection of information unless it displays a currently valid OMB control number.

---

[3] Treatment includes examinations to determine if a serious health condition exists and evaluations of the condition. Treatment does not include routine physical examinations, eye examinations, or dental examinations.

[4] A regimen of continuing treatment includes, for example, a course of prescription medication (*e.g.*, an antibiotic) or therapy requiring special equipment to resolve or alleviate the health condition. A regimen of treatment does not include the taking of over-the-counter medications such as aspirin, antihistamines, or salves; or bed-rest, drinking fluids, exercise, and other similar activities that can be initiated without a visit to a health care provider.

Public Burden Statement

We estimate that it will take an average of 20 minutes to complete this collection of information, including the time for reviewing instructions, searching existing data sources, gathering and maintaining the data needed, and completing and reviewing the collection of information. If you have any comments regarding this burden estimate or any other aspect of this collection of information, including suggestions for reducing this burden, send them to the Administrator, Wage and Hour Division, Department of Labor, Room S-3502, 200 Constitution Avenue, N.W., Washington, D.C. 20210.

DO NOT SEND THE COMPLETED FORM TO THIS OFFICE; IT GOES TO THE EMPLOYEE.

While you're on leave, your employer can contact you to ask your status, but cannot get information from your health care provider without your permission. You can't be required to return to "light duty" work unless this is something you choose to do. The use of a FMLA leave cannot be counted against you when hiring, a promotion, a bonus, or disciplinary actions or decisions are made. While on leave you must be allowed to accrue benefits and seniority.

For more information about FMLA, see *www.dol.gov/esa/whd/fmla*. To contact the U.S. Department of Labor with questions or violations, reach them at 1-866-4-USWAGE.

State Family Leave Laws

Although the federal law does not apply to same-sex spouses, several states have their own family leave laws that allow employees to take time off to care for an ill partner.

California

California state family leave act allows gay partners to take off up to six weeks of paid leave (55 percent of your salary or $728 per week, whichever is lower) to care for a seriously ill registered domestic partner or child born to a registered domestic partner. Only businesses with 50 or more employees must guarantee that an employee's job will be waiting when they return. For more information contact the Employment Development Department (EDD) at *www.edd.ca.gov* or 1-877-BE-THERE.

Connecticut

Couples who have obtained a Connecticut civil union are eligible for the state family leave law. To qualify you must work for an employer with 75 employees or more and have worked 1,000 hours in the previous 12 months. You can take up to 16 weeks of unpaid leave in a two-year period to care for your partner with a serious illness.

For more information contact the Wage and Workplace Standards Division at (860) 263-6790 or *www.ctdol.state.ct.us/index.htm*.

Hawaii

Hawaii state leave law applies to companies with 100 employees or more and provides up to four weeks of unpaid family leave per year to care for a seriously ill reciprocal beneficiary.

For more information, contact the Hawaii Department of Labor at (806) 586-8842 or *http://hawaii.gov/labor*.

Oregon

The Oregon Family Leave Act applies to employers who employ at least 25 employees in Oregon for 20 or more weeks in the current or preceding calendar years. Employees can take up to12 weeks of unpaid leave in a year to care for a seriously ill partner.

For more information, contact the Oregon Bureau of Labor and Industry at (971) 673-0761 or *www.boli.state.or.us*.

Vermont

Couples who have a Vermont civil union are eligible for the state family leave law. The law applies to companies with 15 or more employees. You must have averaged 30 hours per week at your job to qualify. The law permits 12 weeks of unpaid leave in a 12 month period.

For more information contact the Vermont Department of Labor at *www.labor.vermont.gov* or (802) 828-4000

Washington, D.C.

The District of Columbia has a medical leave law that applies to employers with 20 or more employees. An employee is entitled to a total of 16 workweeks of family leave during any 24-month period to care for a seriously ill domestic partner.

For more information contact:

Government of the District of Columbia

Citywide Call Center

John A. Wilson Building

1350 Pennsylvania Avenue, NW

Washington, D.C. 20004

(202) 727-1000

Individual Employer Policies

According to a survey done by the Human Rights Foundation, 72 percent of Fortune 500 companies offer family leave to domestic partners to care for a child or a partner. To find out if your company offers family leave, check your employee or union handbook, or ask your union representative or human resources department if you can find the answer on your own.

Creative Options

If you need time off to care for a partner, but your employer does not provide it, there are other solutions to consider. A first choice would be to use vacation and personal time. If you are able to financially afford it, an unpaid leave (outside the provisions of FMLA) can work for you. If you are considering such an unpaid leave, you will need to carefully specify how long you will be gone and you want to make sure that you have job security. You may be required to pay the cost of your health insurance benefits during the time you are absent from work.

You may be able to work out an arrangement with your employer in which you reduce your hours, work from home part of the time, or change job responsibilities which allow you to be more flexible in your hours. Flex time is an option—you work the same number of hours but can do so on a flexible schedule. For example, you could work four 10 hour days, or stay late on some days to make up for leaving early on others. Job sharing is another possibility to consider. Job sharing usually entails cutting your hours and sharing the responsibilities of one job with another person. If you want to propose job sharing, first determine if it has ever been done in your company before. It is best to present your supervisor with a complete plan, so try to line up someone who is interested in job sharing with you and have some preliminary talks about responsibilities. When you present the plan to your supervisor, you will want to show that it won't be an inconvenience to the company and that just as much work, if not more, will be done under the new arrangement. Job sharing often ends up being more expensive for employers if both job sharers receive benefits (such as health insurance), so be sure to emphasize the benefits to the company and how those costs are offset.

If you work for a small company or business, your best bet is to sit down with your supervisor or boss and explain your situation and why you need some time off. You can make this an "issue" (which of course has the benefit of calling attention to the vast inequities facing same-sex couples), but you can also just make this a personal matter—one human to another—and play upon his or her sympathies.

Coordinating Leaves

If you qualify for several types of leave (for example federal FMLA and state family leave for your own illness, or state leave in addition to company-provided leave to care for a partner), it is important to talk to your human resources contact to determine the best order in which to take your leaves. Don't forget to factor in available vacation or personal time, as well as leave you may qualify for under paid state or employer-funded disability policies when dealing with your own illness. You should also ask about what forms you need to complete to apply for the different types of leaves as well as what documentation (such as from a physician) is required. Keep copies of all paperwork and keep a log of conversations you have with your boss or human resource contact about your options and decisions.

Chapter 9

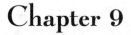

Post-Life Issues

Whether you are facing the loss of a partner or spouse, or making plans for your own passing, post-life decisions can be difficult and challenging, especially when they are made during grief and stress. Planning ahead can allow you to make decisions in advance, at a time when you may be better able to weigh the options.

These are issues that may not be fun to think about, but if you can consider your own wishes now and discuss wishes with your partner, if you have one, you will both be fully informed and prepared to make these decisions, should you ever need to. If one of you is ill, talking about these issues and working through them can be a relief to all involved.

Organ Donations

The issue of organ donations by gay men has received some media attention lately. There has been a lot of confusion about what the rule is. Recently, gay actor and activist Albert Soto chose to donate his organs but they were not accepted. The national policy on organ donations does not exclude gay donors. However, the wiggle room exists at the point of the organs being evaluated and chosen for use. The facility accepting the organs can turn them down for a lack of suitability and this can include donors who have had sex with other men in the past five years.

If you want to be an organ donor, sign the back of your driver's license or get an organ donor card, which looks similar to this (go to *www.organdonor.gov* to find out more):

Organ/Tissue Donor Card

I wish to donate my organs and tissues. I wish to give:

☐ any needed organs and tissues ☐ only the following organs and tissues:

Donor
Signature _____ Date _____

Witness _____

Witness _____

If you want to be an organ donor, it is also important that you discuss this wish with your partner or family members. The decision to donate organs often must be done on the spot and if you want your wishes carried out, it is important to make them known. When you donate organs, your family or partner will still have a body to bury or cremate in most situations.

For more information about organ donations, visit *www.organdonor.gov*, where you can download an organ donor card or request hard copies of organ donor cards.

Medical Research Donations

If you would like to be an organ donor, but believe your donation will not be accepted or used, there is another similar option to consider. You can donate your body to research, so that it can be used by medical students or researchers. If you are interested in doing so, contact a medical school in your area. Ask if they have such a program and what the details are. They will send you some paperwork to read and complete. If you decide to proceed, sign the consent form. There will most likely be a form to keep with your will and other important documents that authorizes transfer of the body upon your death. Make sure your partner or family is aware of your decision so there is no delay in locating the paperwork or your body being transported.

Some medical schools will cremate the remains when they are done and return the ashes to the family or loved ones. Determine what the policy is in advance, so everyone knows what to expect.

The Uniform Anatomical Gifts Act is a law in place in each state governing the treatment of donated bodies. There has been recent coverage in the media about the lack of care and respect that is sometimes used with cadavers at medical schools and research facilities, so if this is something you are concerned about, you should check with the medical school in which you are interested to discuss its policies.

You can also decide to donate a partner's body after his or her death without his or her prior consent, unless other arrangements have already been directed by him or her. This choice would be made by the person considered to have the legal right to dispose of the body—next of kin, which includes partners in some states. (See later in this chapter for more information about this.)

There is a useful book, now out of print, but available used, called *Anatomical Gift: Whole Body Donation Guide* by Regina Lee, which discusses this topic and includes details of programs at many medical schools.

Autopsies

The next of kin has the authority to make decisions about autopsies or post-mortem exams. In Massachusetts, Vermont, Connecticut, Hawaii, and California, you have the right to make this decision for your partner. If the authorities believe a crime was involved with the death, an autopsy can be ordered without the consent of the next of kin.

You can include a section in your health care directive that authorizes your partner to make autopsy decisions for you, but this may not be valid in all states. A provision in your will is generally not effective because it is read too late to have any impact.

Obituary Notices

Many traditional newspapers will not include the name of a partner in an obituary. If having a partner mentioned is important to you, consider placing an obituary in your local GLBT paper. You can also write one for a partner yourself and circulate it by e-mail, or put it on a blog or Webpage, along with photos of the deceased as a memorial.

It is also possible to write your own obituary before your death and leave it for your loved ones to use. Most newspapers have a set format for free obituaries and also offer longer obituaries (often with a photo) for a fee, in which more details can be included.

Funerals

Anyone can hold a funeral or memorial service. Disposition of the body is a different matter (see the next section on burial and cremation). While most people prefer to have one united plan for a funeral or memorial, it is not unusual for partners and friends to hold one separately (usually without the body present) from the one planned by the family if there is a rift. If you, as the partner of the deceased, are not welcome at the one planned by the family, or if you do not agree with the manner in which it is being held, you can hold your own whenever and wherever you wish without interference from them. If you are in the situation where you are not welcome at the service held by the family, simply doing nothing at all to memorialize your loved one can cause more harm than good. You need to find a way to actively grieve and work through the situation. Planning your own event, even if it is something simple at your apartment with a few friends, can help you work through the stages of grief, and provide you with the support of others which you need at a difficult time.

It is possible to plan your own funeral or memorial in advance. You can include instructions in your will (be sure others know this if you do so because a will is not usually read until after the funeral) or create a separate notarized document setting out your wishes. You can prepay for a funeral and make all the arrangements in advance so it is settled and paid for.

It is important to make sure you specify that your partner is the person who will have the authority to make all of the decisions for your funeral (if you do not preplan it), so that he or she is not excluded. This will control the funeral or memorial that which your body is present, but does not prevent others from holding a separate ceremony.

When planning a funeral, you should be aware of the Federal Funeral Law, which regulates the amount and type of information funeral homes must give those purchasing products and services. This law is especially important if you wish to purchase the very minimum, because many funeral homes try to up-sell whenever possible, so knowing your rights can help you get what you want. Reading this information in advance and keeping it in the back of your head is a good idea because when you are dealing with grief you often do not focus on issues or do not have time to begin to researching your rights. If you know in advance your rights under the law, you can recall it, or quickly look it up, in your time of need.

The law requires that funeral homes:

✚ Provide a written price list or offer one over the phone when requested.

✚ Inform you that embalming (a significant expense) is not required in most cases (however, if the body is not embalmed, direct burial or cremation is necessary).

✚ Notify you of fees for items they rent or purchase, as well as service fees for these items, and itemize these fees on your statement.

✚ Make a cardboard or canvas casket substitute available if you prefer. Wooden or metal caskets are not required by any kind of law or regulation and are quite expensive. This is an expense some people choose to skip, particularly if you are going to be using cremation.

✚ Allow you to choose only the products and services you want—you can't be locked in to only choosing from certain inclusive packages.

✚ Disclose laws about funerals that apply in your state.

✚ Provide an itemized statement for all products and services.

✚ Give truthful information about how long a procedure will actually preserve a body and how watertight a casket is.

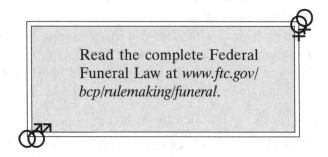

Read the complete Federal Funeral Law at *www.ftc.gov/ bcp/rulemaking/funeral*.

Burial and Cremation

Next of kin has the right to make decisions about what will happen to the body of the deceased. In Massachusetts, Vermont, Connecticut, California, and Maine, that right goes to the partner or spouse. In other states, next of kin does not include a same-sex partner. You can include instructions about your burial or cremation wishes in your will or in a separate notarized document and authorize your partner as the one with decision-making authority. But just as with funeral instructions, it is important that people know about it in advance so that your wishes can be followed.

It is also possible, as discussed in Chapter 6, to use cremation and then divide the remains among two groups of people, so that each can have their own ceremony and closure.

Donations in Lieu of Flowers

Many people prefer to ask for donations in lieu of flowers for a funeral. If you or a partner would like to do this, you can think about it in advance, and consider the various organizations you might be interested in having donations go to. You can contact the organization in advance if you wish, to find out how the funds are used and what kind of recordkeeping they employ. Many charitable organizations handle these memorial donations in a well-organized way, arranging for a thank-you note and tax receipt to go to the donor, as well as a list of donors to the family. You can research this and have a plan in place in advance, or you can simply wait until there is a need and make arrangements then. You will want to know where donations are going before an obituary notice is written though, so this information can be included.

HIV Memorials

HIV memorials are a touching way to not only memorialize a loved one, but to add to awareness of this devastating illness. There are many different HIV/AIDS memorial projects, such as The AIDS Memorial Grove (*www.aidsmemorial.org*), The AIDS Memorial Quilt (*www.aidsquilt.org*), and The International AIDS Candlelight Memorial (*www.candlelightmemorial.org*). They all have different styles or personalities, so choose one that you feel comfortable with. In addition, there are many smaller, community oriented memorials. Participating in a memorial can be a way to honor your loved one's memory and heal yourself. If you want to find a local memorial, contact your local gay pride organization for information.

Transfer of Ownership After the Death of a Partner

After a partner has passed, his or her will needs to go through probate. The executor of the estate is responsible for distributing property in accordance with the terms of the will.

If there is no will, an administrator is appointed to distribute the estate in accordance with intestacy laws. If the estate is small, the administration process is usually expedited. You can hire an attorney to handle this for you, no matter what the size of the estate. Many people feel they are able to handle small estate administration without assistance once they obtain forms and instructions from their local probate court.

If there is property that passes outside of probate (such as jointly held accounts and other joint assets), you generally need to provide a copy of the death certificate to effect a change in ownership.

Bank Accounts

Bank accounts in joint names (or the sole name of the deceased) may be frozen after the death (this varies by state), so if you need access to those funds, it is best to remove some immediately. For this reason, if you are anticipating the death of a partner, it makes sense to maintain a separate individual account so that you aren't in the position of being unable to access funds, even if it is for a short period of time. To unfreeze funds, talk to your bank manager for details on what is required.

Home

If you own a home jointly, you can continue to make payments; if you have mortgage insurance, it will kick in. The deed will need to be changed to reflect the loss of the other owner. You'll need the help of an attorney to handle this. The mortgage will also be changed to reflect this. You can also notify your local property tax authority of the change in ownership.

Cars

If a vehicle was in joint names, you can change the title at your department or commission of motor vehicles. If the car was in the name of the deceased, ownership will need to be passed by will or state intestacy laws. Ownership of a car automatically passes to a surviving spouse (in Massachusetts, Connecticut, and Vermont this applies to same-sex spouses) or surviving children upon death. When there is no spouse or child, transfer of ownership has to be made by the executor or administrator of the estate. In order to continue driving a vehicle your deceased partner owned, you must make sure there is still insurance on it, which means you may have to wait until ownership is transferred. Check with an attorney so you understand your states laws.

Insurance

You will need to notify homeowners, renters, and auto insurance companies of the death, but there is no urgency to this. You'll want to leave insurance in place while ownership is being transferred. You will also need to change the beneficiary on your own life insurance policies, if you had listed your deceased partner as beneficiary.

Safe-Deposit Boxes

You need a court order to open safe-deposit boxes that are solely in the name of the deceased. If you are a joint owner of the box, you can access it.

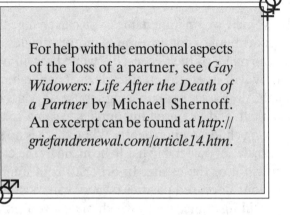

For help with the emotional aspects of the loss of a partner, see *Gay Widowers: Life After the Death of a Partner* by Michael Shernoff. An excerpt can be found at *http://griefandrenewal.com/article14.htm*.

How to Probate a Will

If your partner has a written will, in most cases, you will need to go through a process called probate, in which the will is approved by the court. The provisions of the will are then put into effect by the executor, the person named in the will who is in charge of distributing assets.

If you are indeed your partner's executor, you will have the authority to distribute his or her property according to the will. If you are named as executor, but do not feel you want to or are able to take on this responsibility, the alternate executor named in the will can be appointed by the court (or the court can find someone else willing to take on the responsibility if there is no alternate or the alternate also refuses). An executor is paid a small amount for his or her work.

It is important to select an attorney to represent you throughout the probate process, so that it goes as smoothly and quickly as possible.

Administrating an Estate

If your partner has passed without a will, then his or her property will pass according to state laws. An administrator is appointed to handle the distribution. In most states there is a very easy and simple process for the administration of small estates, for which an attorney is usually not needed, so this may be an option to consider.

Collecting Benefits

If you are the beneficiary under your partner's life insurance, retirement plan, or other benefits, you will need to contact the insurance company that issued the policy and obtain the necessary forms to apply for the benefits. You will most likely need to supply a death certificate with the application (usually available through your local department of vital records or statistics).

Often people have small life insurance policies through their employers, credit cards, credit unions, or other organizations, but because these policies are not directly purchased by them, good records are not kept of these policies. Be sure to check your partner's files for any evidence of this type of policy. You can also check with his or her employer to determine if there was a company-sponsored policy. When you close an account, ask if they can determine whether there was a life insurance policy related to the account.

Bereavement Leave

If you are seeking bereavement leave for the loss of a partner, check with your human resources department or union representative to learn what specific policies apply to your company or position. In the following states, partners are included in the state definition of spouse for the purpose of bereavement leave: California, Connecticut, Delaware, Massachusetts, Oregon, and Vermont. If your company does not have a formal bereavement policy, you can take personal, vacation, or sick time, or you may be able to take "unofficial" bereavement leave, if your employer is sympathetic to your situation.

Grief Counselors

When you lose a loved one, the impact is long-lasting. Finding a grief counselor who can help you work through your feelings and continue to live your life can be an essential step. If you have been working with a hospice organization, they will provide grief counseling for at least one year. If not, seek a referral to a grief counselor who has experience working with same-sex partners.

If you and your partner have minor children, it is equally important that you seek grief counseling for the children. The death of a parent is a devastating, life-changing event. When your child goes through a difficult time, you as the parent are often able to provide help and support, but in the situation where you both suffer a tremendous loss, the parent needs help supporting the children.

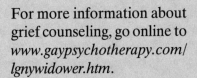

For more information about
grief counseling, go online to
*www.gaypsychotherapy.com/
lgnywidower.htm*.

Chapter 10

Children Are Our Future:

Your Rights in Your Child's Health Care

Becoming a parent is a choice many gays and lesbians make and there are many options available for parenting. Whether you are the legal parent or the nonlegal parent of a child in your home, being involved in educated decisions about your child's health is important to you.

Fertility Treatments

The gayby boom has seen a dramatic increase in the number of gays and lesbians who become parents, many through the use of reproductive procedures, such as insemination, surrogacy, or even IVF. There continues to be some discrimination by these types of specialists, but most are amenable to working with the GLBT population. A recent California case held that a fertility clinic there could not discriminate because of sexual orientation.

When considering a clinic or specialist, it is usually best to ask if they are gay-friendly. Or you can make an appointment and gauge the reactions to you and your partner. If a provider refuses to treat you (and some certainly do, citing "social issues" as the cause of your fertility concern), find someone else. The key is to find a doctor you trust and whom you are comfortable. If you are a lesbian, home insemination is always an option, whether using a known donor or ordering donor sperm by mail from a sperm bank.

Insurance Coverage

The following states mandate some insurance coverage for fertility treatments:

- ✚ Arkansas
- ✚ California
- ✚ Connecticut
- ✚ Hawaii
- ✚ Illinois
- ✚ Maryland
- ✚ Massachusetts
- ✚ Montana
- ✚ New Jersey
- ✚ New York
- ✚ Ohio

- Rhode Island
- Texas
- West Virginia

The amount of coverage will vary by individual policies though, so it is always important to check what is covered and what is not. In most cases, you must receive a diagnosis first, simply saying that you've been trying to conceive for so many months without success. There is no insurance coverage for surrogacy, but lesbians may be able to have insemination, infertility drugs, and other procedures covered.

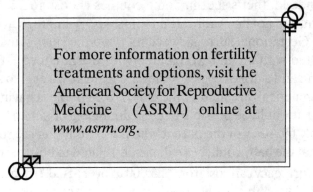

For more information on fertility treatments and options, visit the American Society for Reproductive Medicine (ASRM) online at *www.asrm.org*.

Insemination

When considering insemination, you have two basic options—a known donor or an unknown donor. No matter what kind you select, the key is to make sure the donor has legally surrendered all rights to the child. If you use a sperm bank, this is taken care of by the bank. If you use a known donor, you will need a reproductive rights attorney to prepare an agreement. You always want to make sure a donor provides a complete personal and family health history and is screened for STIs.

It is not illegal to perform an insemination at home, yourself. You also have the option of having the procedure performed by a physician.

Surrogacy

Surrogacy is an option that appeals to male couples. There are two types of surrogacy. In traditional surrogacy, the surrogate's own eggs are used and are inseminated with the intended father's sperm. Some couples choose to mix their sperm and not know for certain whose sperm impregnated the egg. Gestational surrogacy occurs when the surrogate is implanted with an embryo created with the intended father's sperm and a donor egg (not the surrogate's own egg, so she is not genetically related to the child). If a couple is having the child, it would be possible to use a donor egg obtained from a family member of the parent who is not donating the sperm, so that the baby could be biologically related to both partners.

Surrogacy can cost from $25,000 to over $50,000 depending on the difficulty involved with conception, the medical issues present in the pregnancy, and what expenses and costs the intended parents are responsible for under the contract.

States where it is a crime to pay for surrogacy:

- ✠ Michigan
- ✠ New Mexico
- ✠ New York
- ✠ Washington

States where surrogacy contracts are unenforceable (This means you can ask a court to enforce it, however you are free to enter into one, knowing that you will not be able to obtain assistance from the court.):

- Indiana
- Louisiana
- Nebraska
- New York
- North Dakota
- Washington, D.C.

States which recognize surrogacy agreements through laws:

- Arkansas
- Florida: Reasonable compensation is permitted.
- Illinois: Procedure is relatively simple.
- New Hampshire: The intended parent is listed on the first birth certificate but it is not issued for 72 hours after the birth.
- Nevada
- Tennessee
- Texas
- Utah: Only infertile heterosexual married couples may enter into a surrogacy agreement. Surrogates must be financially stable, not on welfare, and must have previously carried and delivered a baby. Surrogacy is not permitted where the embryo is completely donated (not related to either intended parent).

✚ Washington: Only unpaid surrogacy is allowed.

✚ Virginia: Has a pre-birth procedure and allows the intended parent to be listed on the first birth certificate.

States with caselaw about surrogacy:

✚ California: Permits surrogacy.

✚ Kentucky: Prohibits surrogacy programs and payments, but this is largely unenforced.

✚ Massachusetts: A recent case encouraged the legislature to enact laws permitting surrogacy.

✚ Ohio: Has caselaw pertaining to heterosexual-intended parent couples.

✚ Oklahoma: Permits surrogacy but requires the surrogate's husband (if any) to refuse to consent to what it is technically considered an egg donation to her (so that he has no legal obligation to the child).

All other states not listed do not address surrogacy in any way.

California is usually considered the most favorable state for surrogacy because the state allows the intended parent or parents to obtain rights to the child before the birth, removing the uncertainty that can occur after a baby is born and a surrogate has time to reconsider her decision.

If you are considering surrogacy, it is essential that you work with an attorney who has handled surrogacies previously. There are agencies that specialize in matching prospective parents to surrogates. When selecting a surrogate it is essential that she has had children before, that everyone involved receives counseling, that your financial agreement is completely spelled out (and completely conforms to the laws of the state in which you enter into it), and that you and the surrogate reach an understanding about what kind of involvement (if any) she will have with the child.

The largest and most well-known surrogacy agency that serves the gay community, is Growing Generations (*www.growinggenerations.com*).

Other Family Building Options

There are other options available for singles or couples who want to have children or add to their families. Adoption is an excellent choice and offers the options of international adoption, public agency adoption, private agency adoption, or privately arranged adoptions. Becoming a foster parent is another alternative that appeals to some people and allows you to give a home to children who need support and care during a difficult time in their lives.

If you are a lesbian and want to become pregnant but insemination is not successful, there are other, more advanced techniques. Invitro fertilization (IVF) is a choice. You can consider egg donation, in which another woman's egg is fertilized and then implanted in your uterus. If you are part of a couple, you could use your partner's eggs, if she doesn't want to (or is unable to) carry a pregnancy.

Another option is embryo donation. Couples going through advanced fertility procedures are often left with additional embryos from their procedures. If they do not plan to use these embryos in the future, they can donate them for use by other couples. Embryo donors and those receiving the donations are usually matched by the lab—you don't have the freedom of selecting your own in most cases, simply because there is a very limited supply.

Second Parent Adoption

In every state except California, when a same-sex couple has a child, only one partner can become the legal parent first. The other parent must do what is called a second parent adoption. This is the same process used by heterosexual stepparents to become legal parents of their stepchildren. It is a simplified adoption process, but still a legal process that should be handled by an attorney.

The following states permit same-sex second parent adoptions:

- ✚ California
- ✚ Connecticut
- ✚ Illinois
- ✚ Massachusetts
- ✚ New Jersey
- ✚ New York
- ✚ Pennsylvania
- ✚ Vermont
- ✚ Washington, D.C.

The following states have permitted some same-sex second parent adoptions, but have no clear rule:

- ✚ Alabama
- ✚ Alaska
- ✚ Delaware
- ✚ Georgia
- ✚ Hawaii
- ✚ Indiana
- ✚ Iowa
- ✚ Louisiana
- ✚ Maryland
- ✚ Michigan
- ✚ Minnesota
- ✚ Nevada
- ✚ New Hampshire
- ✚ New Mexico
- ✚ Ohio
- ✚ Oregon
- ✚ Rhode Island
- ✚ Texas
- ✚ Washington

Family Leave for Children

If you give birth to a child or adopt a child, you are eligible for the federal Family and Medical Leave Act (see Chapter 7 for details). Additionally, if your child becomes ill and needs care, you can take time for that under this act as well. You will also have rights under your state family and medical leave law.

If you are eligible for both federal and state family leave, you will need to talk to your human resources contact to learn in what order you must take the leaves and if time taken on one leave applies to another. (For example, if you take 12 weeks of FMLA but are allowed 14 weeks under state leave, find out whether the 12 FMLA weeks are subtracted from your available state leave.)

When your spouse or partner gives birth to a child and you are not yet a legal parent, you do not qualify for leave under the federal law, but you may qualify under your state law.

Following are state leave laws that pertain to the birth or adoption of a child. Note that the laws for public employers are sometimes different, so if you work for a state or local government, find out what kind of leave you are entitled to.

Alaska

Private employers with 21 or more employees are required to offer 18 workweeks within a 12 month period for pregnancy and childbirth, or adoption in a 24 month period. A court case has held that the state must extend the same benefits to state employee domestic partners as it does to spouses. This has not yet been implemented.

California

Workers in a domestic partnership receive up to six weeks of benefits within a 12 month period. California family leave is paid leave 55 percent of your salary or $728 per week, whichever is lower. The parent who gives birth to or adopts a child may take a leave, and so can the registered domestic partner of this person. The same job position upon your return is guaranteed if there are 50 or more employees.

Connecticut

To qualify you must be in a civil union and work for an employers of 75 employees or more and have worked 1,000 hours in the previous 12 months. You can take up to 24 weeks of leave in a two year period for the birth or adoption of a child. For more information contact Wage and Workplace Standards Division at (860) 263-6790 or *www.ctdol.state.ct.us/index.htm*.

Hawaii

Companies with 100 employees or more must provide up to four weeks per year for the birth or adoption of a child for parents and reciprocal beneficiaries. For more information, contact the Hawaii Department of Labor at (806) 586-8842 or *http://hawaii.gov/labor*.

Massachusetts

Employers of six or more employees are required to offer eight weeks of leave for the purpose of giving birth or adopting a child. This applies if you have a Massachusetts marriage. For more information contact the Department of Labor at *www.mass.gov/dol* or (617) 788-3610.

Minnesota

Employers of 21 or more are required to offer six weeks of leave for birth or adoption of a child. For more information contact the Department of Labor and Industry at *www.doli.state.mn.us*/or (800) 342-5354.

New Jersey

Employers of 100 or more employees are required to offer no more then 12 weeks for the birth of a child. The state family leave law defines a parent as a biological parent, adoptive parent, stepparent, or someone having a "parent-child relationship." For more information, contact the Department of Labor and Workforce Development at *www.state.nj.us/labor* or (609) 292-7060.

Oregon

The law applies to same-sex couples working for employers who employ at least 25 employees in Oregon for 20 or more weeks in the current or preceding calendar years. Employees can take up to 12 weeks for the birth or adoption of a child. For more information, contact the Oregon Bureau of Labor and Industry at (971) 673-0761 or *www.boli.state.or.us*.

Vermont

The law applies to residents in a civil union working for companies with 15 or more employees. You must have averaged 30 hours per week at your job. The law permits 12 weeks unpaid leave in a 12-month period. For more information contact the Vermont Department of Labor at *www.labor.vermont.gov* or (802) 828-4000.

Washington, D.C.

Employers must offer 16 weeks of family leave during any 24-month period for birth or adoption of a child to domestic partners.

Wisconsin

If you live in a state that allows you to take state family leave for a partner's illness (see Chapter 8 for a list of these states), but does not extend the law to take time off to spend with your partner's new baby, you are able to use the law to take time off to care for your partner if she gives birth.

If you are not entitled to take a family leave, there are other options available to you, such as flex time, job sharing, unpaid leave outside FMLA, reducing your hours, and more. See Chapter 8 for more information about these options.

hours in the previous 12 months. You can take up to 16 weeks of leave in a two-year period to care for a new child.

Child Health Insurance Coverage

If you are the legal parent of your child, you can carry him or her on your health insurance if you have a family policy. If you are not your child's legal parent, but you are able to provide coverage for your partner, then your child will be covered as the child of a dependent.

Another health insurance solution for your family may be state sponsored programs. For more information, see Chapter 3.

If you are both legal parents of your child but do not or cannot have one policy that covers both you and your partner, you'll need to choose one of your two policies to use as a family policy, which will provide coverage for your child. When considering which policy to use, consider the following:

- ✚ Does either policy offer free well-child visits?
- ✚ Is there a lower co-pay for children's doctor visits?
- ✚ What kind of prescription coverage is there for common childhood medications such as amoxicillin?

- ✚ How many physicians are in-network in your area?
- ✚ How many pediatricians and pediatric specialists?
- ✚ Do you need referrals to see specialists?
- ✚ Is there a discount prescription by e-mail program?
- ✚ What kind of mental health coverage is provided?
- ✚ What is the hospital deductible?
- ✚ What is the emergency room deductible?
- ✚ What is the lifetime cap?
- ✚ Is there a yearly overall deductible?
- ✚ Is there dental or vision care included in the policy? What are the co-pays and coverage?
- ✚ What is the employee contribution to the premium?

Once you have the answers to these questions, sit down and compare the two policies and choose the one that makes the most financial sense for your family. Remember that if you are unhappy with the coverage, you can always switch your child over to your partner's policy during open enrollment times.

You need to make a decision about health insurance coverage before your child is born or placed with you. If your child is born to your family, you will need to notify hospital intake personnel as to which policy the baby will be on, particularly if the child will not be on the policy of the person giving birth (the baby is usually automatically added to that policy at birth).

FSAs and HSAs

Chapter 3 discussed Flexible Spending Accounts and Health Savings Accounts. If you are the legal parent of your child, you can use these accounts to pay for his or her medical costs as well as your own.

Rights to Make Medical Decisions

If you are your child's legal parent, you have the absolute authority to make any health care decisions for your child, unless the child is from a previous relationship and the court order says that you specifically do not have this authority.

If you are not a legal parent, it is imperative that the other parent complete a written consent similar to the one below, authorizing you to make health care decisions for your child. You don't want to be in a situation where your partner is away and your child needs health care, but your partner can be reached. Rest assured that emergency room physicians will provide emergency care to save life and limb without parental consent, and many pediatricians will treat their regular patients, no matter who brings the child in. But you don't want there to ever be any question, so it is best to have this authorization signed and ready to go just in case. It is also a good idea to create an authorization similar to this if a relative provides child care for you on a regular basis, so that he or she can obtain medical care if necessary.

I, _____, parent of my child _____, DOB _____, authorize my partner and co-parent _____ to make any and all health care decisions for our child at any time without consulting me.

_____

Signed Date

Notary:

You may wish to execute several of these and give one to your patcian to keep. Another one can be kept in a diaper bag, in a car, in a wallet, or someplace else where it is easily accessible.

Discrimination in Medical Care

Note the American Academy of Pediatrics (AAP, *www.aap.org*) has issued a statement specifically supporting gay parents. In 2002, the Committee on Psychosocial Aspects of Child and Family Health issued a statement saying that they support second parent adoption by gay parents. The statement also said that children raised by gay parents have the same advantages and the same expectations for health, adjustment, and development as children whose parents are heterosexual. It goes on to say that all pediatricians should become familiar with literature about gay parents.

Although this statement is an important one, it cannot eradicate all existing discrimination. If your child's pediatrician is not supportive or has an issue with you being gay, find someone else.

Hospital Visitation

If you are a nonlegal parent, it is also a good idea to have your partner execute a hospital visitation authorization form, allowing you to see your child while in the hospital. Most likely this won't be a problem, but you want to avoid a situation where hospital staff refuses to let you in because you are not immediate family in the traditional sense. Use a form such as this:

> I, _____, parent of the child _____, date of birth _____, hereby authorize my partner _____ to have unrestricted access to our child when he or she is in a hospital, treatment facility, or other health care institution, whether or not I am present.
>
> _____
>
> Signed Date
> Notary:

If your child enters a hospital or other treatment facility in a non-emergency situation, the legal parent should be sure to inform the staff and have it noted on the chart that the other is to have full access to the child and can make medical decisions at any time.

Naming a Guardian

All legal parents should name a guardian for their children in their wills. Even if you and your partner have a union recognized by your state at this time, it is a good idea to first state that you name your partner as guardian, and then select an alternate. When selecting an alternate guardian, choose someone who has a relationship with your child, and who would raise your child in a way of which you would approve. It is a good idea to discuss the potential guardianship with the person you are naming to be sure it is a responsibility he or she would be willing to take on.

The choice of a guardian in your will is not binding on the court, but it is very persuasive. If your partner is not a legal parent, it may be helpful to include an explanation in your will saying that you are raising the child together as co-parents and that your partner is a complete partner in every aspect of your life and is a true parent to your child. If you select an alternate guardian it is a good idea to explain why you have selected this person and what kind of relationship your family has with him or her.

Parenting After the Death of Your Partner

If you and your partner have a minor child together and your partner passes away, one of your primary concerns will be for your child. If you are a legal parent to your child, you have no worries about custody. If, however, you never became a legal parent to your child, things can become complicated.

If the child has another legal parent (such as from a partner's previous relationship) that parent will have a nearly undisputed right to raise the child. You can fight this, but you will need an attorney who is experienced in this type of matter. If there is no other legal parent in the picture, and your partner has named you as guardian in his or her will, a court is very likely to award guardianship to you. The fact that you are gay should play no role in the court's decision, because guardianship is decided on what is best for the child, and if you have been acting in a parental role, you are in a very good position. If there is no will, there will be a hearing to determine who is best suited to care for the child. The court will give weight to blood relatives who seek custody, but your role as an emotional parent (one whom the child sees as a parent) will also be extremely important. Again though, in this kind of situation, it is essential to have a good attorney who is experienced in this type of case.

Chapter 11

Gray Gays and Skirts:

Issues for Seniors and Transgendered Individuals

Two of the most overlooked groups within the GLBT community are seniors and those who are transgendering. If you're in one of these situations, the other sections of this book definitely apply to you, but you may be facing some other specific issues that others are not dealing with. Seniors are usually thinking about the health care options they will have as they age and need more assistance. TG individuals face problems with insurance coverage, as well health care providers who may not be understanding.

Health Insurance Coverage for Transgendering

Transgender medical procedures are excluded from many health insurance policies, however, Aetna, the City of San Francisco policy, and Kaiser Permanante California are companies that provide some or complete coverage. There is a chance your insurance policy may provide some coverage, so it is best to check first before assuming there is no coverage. The lack of coverage is a source of extreme discrimination, because many of the treatments used in transgendering procedures (such as hormone therapy) are covered by insurance when used for other medical purposes. The main reason these procedures are denied coverage is because they are not considered to be medically necessary. Hopefully, the insurance community will realize that transgender procedures are medically necessary for some people and eventually provide coverage. Until then, if this is an issue you are concerned about, you should make your voice heard through local pride groups.

For assistance and support with transgender issues, contact the National Transgender Advocacy Coalition at *www.ntac.org*.

Mental Health Care for Transgendering

Gender Identity Disorder (GID) is classified in the *Diagnostic and Statistical Manual of Mental Disorders*, the basic diagnostic guide used by mental health care professionals. If a health insurance policy provides mental health coverage, this is a diagnosis that will be covered if it is not involved in the actual transgender procedure. So in other words if you're trying to "cure" yourself of it, or cope without surgery, you will have coverage. But if you are actually surgically or pharmaceutically transgendering, it is likely there will be no coverage, but this may be dependant on how your counselor bills it, so be sure to ask if there is a way around this. It's important to note that a lot of people suffer from very generalized mental health problems that can be characterized as anxiety or self-esteem issues; this type of diagnosis could be submitted instead of GID to obtain coverage for mental health services.

To find a counselor or therapist skilled in transgender issues, contact the Association for Gay, Lesbian and Bisexual Issues in Counseling division of the American Counseling Association at *www.aglbic.org/resources/ listing.htm*.

Health Care Discrimination and TG

There are many physicians, health care providers, and hospitals who may be unwilling to provide medical care to transgendered, transsexual, or transgendering individuals.

Gay & Lesbian Medical Rights

There are 70 state and local jurisdictions across the United States that prohibit health care discrimination against transgender individuals, by public hospitals or health care institutions, including these states:

- ✚ California
- ✚ Connecticut
- ✚ Hawaii
- ✚ Illinois
- ✚ Maine
- ✚ Massachusetts
- ✚ Minnesota
- ✚ New Jersey
- ✚ New Mexico
- ✚ New York
- ✚ Rhode Island
- ✚ Washington, D.C.

If you have no formal protection from discrimination in your state, it is important that you still point out discriminatory treatment you have faced. Report it to the practice the health care provider is a member of, or to the hospital or clinic where you were treated. Many of these businesses may have formal anti-discriminatory policies and most of them don't want to lose business and will listen to your complaints. This is also an excellent way to raise awareness of this issue.

In addition to discrimination for the actual transgender process, it is not uncommon for TG individuals to be denied coverage for other unrelated medical problems because the insurance company decides these other health issues are related to the transgender process. If this happens you, it is essential that you get an attorney and fight it. A 2001 California case (*Jane Doe v. Diana M. Bonta*) held that insurance companies cannot have a blanket policy denying any treatment to TG individuals and must evaluate all patients and treatments on a case-by-case basis.

Another type of discrimination is caused by the rigid categories the medical system has in place. Every person must identify him- or herself as male or female and if you identify yourself as male, you can't get coverage for gynecological problems. For more information, visit *www.transgenderlaw.com*.

Chapter 1 discussed domestic violence laws and shelters, but this is an even more difficult issue for TG and transsexual individual. For more information, visit *www.survivorproject.org*.

Physicians and Transgendering

Finding a physician to treat you when you are TG can be difficult. If you are seeking a physician to work with you through the transgender process, you need to locate a specialist. Many physicians will not work with a transgendering person without a letter from a therapist explaining that the person has carefully thought it out and discussed it, and the procedure would be in his or her best interest.

If you are already through the transgender process, it can be difficult to locate a primary physician who will treat you. A physician can refuse to treat you, and if you are looking for a new doctor, your best plan is to call the office and ask if he or she will treat a transgendered person. You can also schedule a consultation visit and judge for yourself based upon the reaction you receive. The International Foundation for Gender Education maintains a list of treating physicians on their Website, *www.ifge.org*.

Information about gender change documents is available online at *www.transgenderlaw.org/resources/index.htm#identity*.

Gay Senior Issues

There are more than 3 million seniors who are gay or lesbian, and with the baby boomers aging, that number is expected to top 6 million. Gay seniors face not only the same kind of discrimination that affects other members of the community, but are also faced with ageism both in the general population and the GLBT community. Gay seniors also tend to feel isolated from the mainstream gay community because of their ages.

Gay-Friendly Senior Care

The majority of gay seniors live alone (not in any kind of assisted living arrangement), because there is often a lack of family support. Many eventually need living assistance as they age or as their health conditions change. If you're a senior, or will be one soon, devising a plan for your health care and living arrangements as you age should be something you carefully consider.

Gay seniors who want to live in a housing community or assisted living arrangement may be more comfortable living in a senior community that is specifically designed for "gray gays." Palms of Manasota in Palmetto, Florida was the first specially designed community of this kind, but since it was built, many more have sprung up around the country. Check with your local pride organization to determine if there is a community near you.

Read about specific issues affecting senior gays and lesbians in the Policy Institute of the National Gay and Lesbian Task Force Foundation's report Outing Age online at *www.thetaskforce.org/downloads/outingage.pdf*.

In many states, gay partners do not have the automatic right to room together in nursing homes as married couples do, creating a great demand for long-term care or continuing care communities where partners can continue to live together.

If you are unable to live in a facility that caters to gay seniors, there are some steps you can take to ensure that a facility or residence you are considering is gay-friendly.

- ✛ Ask if the lease or contract has an anti-discrimination policy that includes sexual orientation.
- ✛ Find out if housing and service staff must receive training in diversity that includes sexual orientation and gender identity.
- ✛ Learn if there are specific staff members who handle gay and lesbian issues.
- ✛ Determine if the staff and residents have access to GLBT health services and community resources.
- ✛ Inquire whether partners can be included in family councils and in decision-making about the resident's health.
- ✛ Make sure partners and GLBT friends are welcome at the facility and at social events.

Always be sure to drop in for an unannounced visit at any nursing home or facility you are considering. The number of Medicaid beds is also an important consideration if you will be relying on Medicaid to pay for your expenses. Ask to meet the social director or social worker in charge of planning activities and get a feel for whether this person has sensitivity to gay issues. Ask to see the three most recent state surveys or inspections of the facility (the nursing home does have these on file). Other important issues in evaluating a nursing home are:

- ✛ The employee-to-resident ratio.
- ✛ Whether patients with Alzheimer's or dementia are in a separate care unit.
- ✛ What the daily schedule is like.
- ✛ How many RNs are on duty at any time.
- ✛ The ratio of RNs to other staff.
- ✛ The total number of patients.

- The types and frequency of activities.
- Whether single rooms are available.
- What the visiting hours are.
- What items residents can bring with them.
- The type of security in place.
- Details about all costs, including additional things such as laundry.

Warning signs include:
- Restraints.
- Odors.
- Listless residents.
- Lack of privacy.
- Secrecy by the staff.
- Judgmental or unfriendly staff members.
- Immediate negative reactions if gay issues are discussed.

There have been many reported incidents of discrimination in nursing homes against gay and lesbian residents, such as aides refusing to wash a lesbian patient. A survey conducted in New York State in 1994 found that gay seniors were not welcome at more than 46 percent of the nursing homes surveyed. This type of discrimination is especially disturbing because it impacts those who are weak or ill. If you or someone you know experiences discrimination in a nursing home or assisted living community, first speak to the employee's supervisor and go up the ladder until you get an answer you like. If necessary go to the nursing home's board of trustees. If you make no headway within the building, you need to contact your state long-term care home ombudsman—a state employee who evaluates and inspects nursing homes in your area.

These employees work to keep nursing homes safe and user-friendly and are there to help nursing home residents with concerns about the care they are receiving. You can find contact information for your ombudsman online at *www.nccnhr.org/static_pages/ombudsmen.cfm* or by checking the government guide section of your phone book.

Become involved in the residents' and family council so that you can have a voice in the way policies are made. You may also wish to get in touch with the National Citizen's Coalition for Nursing Home Reform at *www.nccnhr.org* or (202) 332-2275.

Always read the entire contract and ask to see it before admission. The person who will be moving into the facility is the person who must sign the contract, unless someone else has power of attorney for her or him.

There are alternatives to senior housing that many seniors (both gay and straight) consider, and often choose. These include living with a family member or friend or obtaining in-home health care and other assistance in order to stay in their own homes. In the San Francisco Bay Area, there are home care services that specifically provide services to gays and lesbians and there may be more around the country.

There is also a developing trend of seniors who share a common interest creating in their own housing community by buying mobile homes next to each other or buying small neighboring homes and knocking down fences. Some even build or buy a central community building.

For more information contact
any of these sources:

GLBT Elder Housing Programs
A Place for US Foundation
Westlake, OH
(440) 899-1475

Arbours at City Center
Fort Lauderdale, FL

Care Consortium
Huntington Valley, PA
(215) 657-9990 ex 218

Cluster Housing Project
East Lansing, MI
(517) 336-0231

GLARP Housing Project
Palm Springs, CA
(310) 966-1500
www.gaylesbianretiring.org

Our Town
San Francisco, CA
www.ourtownvillages.com

Palms of Manasota, Inc.
Palmetto, FL
(941) 722-5858
www.prideworks.com/palms.htm

Queen City Development Corporation
Seattle, WA
www.seattlegayculture.org

Rainbow Adult Community Housing
3890 24th Street
San Francisco, CA 94114
(415) 285-4307

Stonewall Communities
PO Box 990035
Prudential Center
Boston, MA 02199
(617) 369-9090

RACH Project
San Francisco, CA
(415) 281-0800

Rainbow Vision Properties
Sante Fe, NM
(212) 989-3573

The Resort on Carefree Boulevard
Fort Myers, FL (800) 326-0364
www.resortoncb.com

Lesbian and Gay Aging Issues Network
(415) 974-9600
www.asaging.org

Services and Advocacy for
GLBT Elders (SAGE)
(212) 741-2247
www.sageusa.org

To locate gay-friendly housing, do a search for gay-friendly senior housing at *www.hrc.org* in the family section, under aging, or visit *www.graygay.com* and click on links.

The Administration on Aging advocates for all seniors, including GLBT seniors. They can be reached at (202) 619-7501 or *www.aoa.gov*.

California's Gray Gay Tax Break

Under the California Domestic Partner law, a registered partner will be excluded from property reassessment when a partner is added or removed from the title (by choice or by death). This is a significant tax break. When a property is reassessed, its value usually goes up, which results in higher property taxes. This law prevents that from happening and is of great benefit to seniors who live on fixed incomes. To qualify though, you must contact your local assessor and complete a form which must remain on file.

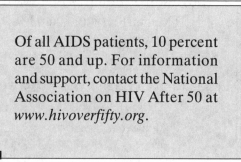

Of all AIDS patients, 10 percent
are 50 and up. For information
and support, contact the National
Association on HIV After 50 at
www.hivoverfifty.org.

Medicaid

Medicaid is the insurance of last resort for many Americans,
and to qualify you must meet financial requirements. Many
people end up "spending down" to Medicaid, where they use
up their existing assets to pay for medical care until they become
eligible for Medicaid. As part of the regulations surrounding
Medicaid, when a husband or wife spends down to Medicaid,
the home is not required to be sold in order to spend down to
reach eligibility. However, this rule only applies to heterosexual married couples, so gay couples must carefully consider this and how to compensate for it. You can't simply
transfer ownership of the home and then go into a nursing
home. Medicaid has a "look back" provision that looks at all
of your assets and transfers within the past three years. If you
and your partner are widely apart in age (say 30 and 50 for
example), it might make sense to transfer ownership of the
home to the younger partner now so that you will be able to
avoid look back when the oldest partner becomes old enough
to need Medicaid.

Planning for the Future

When you and your partner do financial planning, making arrangements to support yourselves when you are older and need medical care is probably one of your primary concerns. Unfortunately this kind of planning is much more difficult for gay couples than for straight, married couples. Gay couples are not entitled to receive Social Security payments through their partner as married couples are. Because of Medicaid rules, it is difficult to determine how to handle home ownership, as well as ownership of other assets. Retirement plans, pension plans, and 401(k)s discriminate against same-sex couples and do not offer the same benefits married heterosexual couples have.

Because of all of these issues, it is essential that domestic partners meet with a financial planner and develop a complete plan to help maximize assets, while sheltering them from Medicaid. Financial planning for a gay couple is more complicated than for heterosexual couples, so it is important to find a financial planner who is experienced not only in Medicaid issues and retirement planning, but also in maximizing gay couples' assets. Find an experienced financial planner through Pride Planners Association at *www.prideplanners.org*.

Other Resources for gay seniors include:

(GLARP) Gay and Lesbian Association of Retired Persons
PO Box 30808
Los Angeles, CA 90024
www.gaylesbianretiring.org

International Longitudinal
Transgender and Transsexual
Aging Research Institute
PO Box 28089
Richmond, VA 23228-28089
(804) 421-2428

(LGAIN) Lesbian and Gay Aging
Issues Network,
American Society on Aging
833 Market Street, Suite 511
San Francisco, CA 94103-1824
(415) 974-9600
www.asaging.org/lgain.html

Resources

Books

Berkery, Peter. *J.K. Lasser's Gay Finances in a Straight World: A Comprehensive Financial Planning Handbook*. Hoboken, N.J.: John Wiley Publishing, 1998.

Bettinger, Michael. *It's Your Hour: A Guide to Queer Affirmative Psychotherapy*. Los Angeles, Calif.: Alyson Publications, 2001.

Chambers, Joyce. *The Easy Will and Living Will Kit: A Simple Plan Everyone Should Have*. Naperville, Ill.: Sourcebooks, 2005

Clunis, Merilee. *The Lesbian Parenting Book*. Emeryville, Calif.: Seal Press, 2003.

Donnelly, Katherine Fair. *Recovering from the Loss of a Loved One to AIDS:Help for Surviving Family, Friends, and Lovers Who Grieve*. New York: Fawcett Books, 2005.

Grodeck, Brett. *The First Year—HIV: An Essential Guide for the Newly Diagnosed*. New York: Marlowe and Company, 2003.

Haman, Edward. *How to Write Your Own Living Will*. Naperville, Ill: Sourcebooks, 2004.

————. *Power of Attorney Handbook*. Naperville, Ill.: Sourcebooks, 2004.

Hardin, Kimeron. *Queer Blues: The Lesbian and Gay Guide to Overcoming Depression*. Oakland, Calif.: New Harbinger, 2001.

Lee, Regina. *Anatomical Gift: Whole Body Donation Guide*. Fayetteville, N.C.: Consumer Education Services, 1997.

Lorig, Kate. *Living Well With HIV and AIDS*. Boulder, Colo.: Bull Publishing, 2000.

Loukes, Keith. *Ask Dr. Keith: Candid Answers To Queer Questions*. Toronto, Canada: Whitecap Books, 2005.

McGarry, Kevin. *Fatherhood for Gay Men: An Emotional and Practical Guide to Becoming a Gay Dad*. San Francisco, Calif.: Harrington Park Press, 2003.

Menichiello, Michael. *A Gay Couple's Journey Through Surrogacy: Intended Fathers*. Binghampton, N.Y.: Haworth Press, 2006.

Mohler, Marie. *A Donor Insemination Guide*. San Francisco, Calif.:Harrington Park Press, 2002.

Pepper, Rachel. *The Ultimate Guide to Pregnancy for Lesbians: Tips and Techniques from Conception to Birth:How to Stay Sane and Care for Yourself*. San Francisco: Cleis, 1999.

Rolcik, Karen Ann. *Living Trusts and Other Ways to Avoid Probate*. Naperville, Ill.: Sourcebooks, 2004.

Rubenstein, William. *The Rights of People Who Are HIV Positive: The Authoritative ACLU Guide to the Rights of People Living With HIV Disease and AIDS*. Carbondale, Ill.: Southern Illinois University Press, 1996.

Sember, Brette. *Gay & Lesbian Legal Rights: A GLBT Guide for Singles, Couples, and Families*. Naperville, Ill.: Sourcebooks, 2006.

—————. *Gay and Lesbian Parenting Choices: From Adopting or Using a Surrogate to Choosing the Perfect Father*. Franklin Lakes, N.J.: Career Press, 2006.

Shalit, Peter. *Living Well: The Gay Man's Essential Health Guide*. Los Angeles, Calif.: Alyson Publications, 1998.

Shernoff, Michael. *Gay Widowers: Life After the Death of a Partner*. Binghampton, N.Y.: Haworth Press, 1997.

Silva, David Wayne. *A Grief Recovery Guide for Gay Men by David Wayne Silva*. West Conshohocken, Pa.: Infinity Publishing, 2000.

Toevs, Kim. *The Essential Guide to Lesbian Conception, Pregnancy, and Birth*. Los Angeles, Calif.: Alyson Publications, 2002.

Wolfe, Daniel. *Men Like Us: The GMHC Complete Guide to Gay Men's Sexual, Physical, and Emotional Well-Being*. New York: Ballantine Books: 2000.

Ziegler, Stacy. *Pathways To Parenthood: The Ultimate Guide To Surrogacy*. Boca Raton, Fla.: Brown Walker Press, 2004.

Organizations

Administration on Aging
www.aoa.gov
(202) 619-7501

AIDS Memorial Grove
www.aidsmemorial.org

AIDS Memorial Quilt
www.aidsquilt.org

American Academy of HIV Medicine
www.aahivm.org
(202) 659-0699

American Academy of Pediatrics (AAP)
www.aap.org
(847) 434-4000

American Red Cross
www.redcross.org
(800) 435-7669

American Medical Association GLBT Advisory Committee
www.ama-assn.org/go/glbt

American Society for Reproductive Medicine (ASRM)
www.asrm.org
(205) 978-5000

Association for Gay, Lesbian, and Bisexual Issues in Counseling Division of the American Counseling Association
www.aglbic.org/resources/listing.htm

Association of Gay and Lesbian Psychiatrists (AGLP)
www.aglp.org
(215) 222-2800

Avon Breast Care Program
www.AvonBreastCare.org

Equal Employment Opportunity Commission
www.eeoc.gov
(800) 669-4000

Gay and Lesbian Association of Retired Persons (GLARP)
www.gaylesbianretiring.org
(310) 709-8743

Gay and Lesbian International Therapist Search Engine
www.glitse.com

Gay and Lesbian Medical Association
www.glma.org
(415) 255-4547

Gay Men's Health Crisis (GMHC)
www.gmhc.org
(212) 367-1000

Growing Generations (surrogacy)
www.growinggenerations.com
(323) 965-7500

HIV Criminal Law and Policy Project
www.hivcriminallaw.org

Human Rights Campaign
www.hrc.org
(202) 628-4160

International AIDS Candlelight Memorial
www.candlelightmemorial.org

International Association of Physicians in AIDS Care (IAPAC)
www.iapac.org
(312) 795-4930

International Foundation for Gender Education
www.ifge.org
(781) 899-2212

International Longitudinal Transgender and Transsexual Aging Research Institute
(804) 421-2428

Joint Commission on Accreditation of Healthcare Organizations (JCAHO)
www.jcaho.org
(800) 994-6610
complaint@jcaho.org

Lambda Legal
www.lambdalegal.org
(212) 809-8585

Lesbian and Gay Aging Issues Network
www.asaging.org
(415) 974-9600

Lesbian Health Fund
www.glma.org/programs/lhf/index.shtml

Maternal and Child Health Services
https://performance.hrsa.gov/mchb/mchreports/link/state_links.asp

Mautner Project for Lesbians with Cancer
www.mautnerproject.org
(202) 332-5536

Medical Information Bureau
www.mib.com

Medicare
www.Medicare.gov

Minority AIDS Project
www.map.org
(800) 225-8550

National Association of Gay and
Lesbian Addiction Professionals
www.nalgap.org
(703) 465-0539

National Association on HIV After 50
www.hivoverfifty.org

National Association of People With AIDS (NAPWA)
www.napwa.org
(240) 247-0880

National Breast and Cervical Cancer
Early Detection Program (NBCCEDP)
www.cdc.gov/cancer/nbccedp/contacts.htm
1-888-842-6355

National Center for HIV, STD, and TB Prevention (NCHSTP)
www.cdc.gov/nchstp/od/nchstp.html

National Citizen's Coalition for Nursing Home Reform
www.nccnhr.org
(202) 332-2275

National Council of Trust and Estate Attorneys
www.actec.org

The National Domestic Violence Hotline
www.ndvh.org
(800) 799-7233

National Eating Disorders Association
www.eatingdisorders.org
(800) 931-2237.

National Hospice and Palliative Care Organization
www.nhpco.org
(800) 658-8898

National Foundation for Credit Counseling
www.nfcc.org
(800) 388-2227

National Lesbian and Gay Law Association
www.nlgla.org
(202) 637-6384

National Minority AIDS Council
www.nmac.org
(202) 483-6622

National Transgender Advocacy Coalition
www.ntac.org

Pride Planners Association (financial planners)
www.prideplanners.org

Ryan White CARE Act
http://hab.hrsa.gov
1-888-275-4772

Services and Advocacy for GLBT Elders (SAGE)
www.sageusa.org
(212) 741-2247

Social Security Administration
www.ssa.gov

Stop AIDS Project
www.stopaids.org

Suicide Hotlines
www.suicidehotlines.com
1-800-SUICIDE
1-800-273-TALK.

UCSF Center for Lesbian Health Research
http://nurseweb.ucsf.edu/iha/les-rsch.htm
(415) 502-5209

U.S. Living Will Registry
www.uslivingwillregistry.com

Websites

Assisted Suicide
www.finalexit.org

CDC's Hepatitis Vaccine: What You Need to Know pamphlet
www.cdc.gov/nip/publications/VIS/vis-hep-a.pdf

Child Abuse Reporting
www.childhelp.com/report_local.htm

Clinical Trials
www.clinicaltrials.gov
international trials are available at *www.centerwatch.com*

Credit Reports
www.annualcreditreport.com

Disability Insurance
www.glad.org/rights/Disability_Benefits.pdf

Domestic Partner Health Insurance Benefits
www.hrc.org/worknet

Domestic Violence State Coalitions
www.ncadv.org/resources/state.htm

Domestic Violence Information
http://gaynorfolk-net.norfolk.on.ca/life-on-brians-beat/
samesexviolence.html www.rainbowdomesticviolence.itgo.com

Family and Medical Leave Act information
www.dol.gov/esa/whd/fmla/

Family and Medical Leave Act medical form
www.dol.gov/esa/regs/compliance/whd/fmla/wh380.pdf

Federal Funeral Law
www.ftc.gov/bcp/rulemaking/funeral

Flexible Spending Accounts
www.irs.gov/publications/p969/ar02.html#d0e1695

Free Clinics
www.freeclinic.net

Gray Gays (seniors)
www.graygay.com
www.thetaskforce.org/downloads/outingage.pdf

Grief
www.gaypsychotherapy.com/lgnywidower.htm

Health Care Proxy Sample
www.palliativecare.org/advancedirectives/healthcareproxy.pdf

Health Care Savings Accounts
www.irs.gov/publications/p969/ar02.html#d0e1695

Health Insurance High Risk Pools
www.healthinsurance.org/riskpoolinfo.html

HIV Health Care
www.aidsinfo.nih.gov
www.thebody.com

HIV Home Testing
www.homeaccess.com

HIV Housing
www.hud.gov/offices/cpd/aidshousing/local/index.cfm

HIV Test Sites
http://hivtest.org/subindex.cfm?FuseAction=Locate

Hospital Rights
www.aha.org/aha/ptcommunication/partnership/index.html

Lesbian Health
www.4woman.gov/faq/lesbian.htm
www.lesbianstd.com

Living Trusts
www.ftc.gov/bcp/conline/pubs/services/livtrust.htm

Living Wills
www.euthanasia.com/lw.html
www.uslivingwillregistry.com/forms.shtm

Medical Record Copying Fees
www.lamblawoffice.com/medical-records-copying-charges.html

Men Who Have Sex With Men Health Information
www.cdc.gov/ncidod/diseases/hepatitis/msm

Nursing Home Ombudsman List
www.nccnhr.org/static_pages/ombudsmen.cfm

Oregon's Death With Dignity Act
http://egov.oregon.gov/DHS/ph/pas/faqs.shtml

Organ Donations
www.organdonor.gov

Prescription drug assistance
www.disabilityresources.org/RX.html
www.atdn.org/access/states/

Social Security for People Living With HIV/AIDS
www.ssa.gov/pubs/10019.pdf

State Health Insurance Information
www.insurekidsnow.gov

Transgendering
www.transgenderlaw.com
www.transgenderlaw.org/resources/index.htm#identity

Transgender Domestic Violence
www.survivorproject.org

U.S. AIDS Drugs Assistance Programs
www.thebody.com/financial/adap.html

U.S. HIV/AIDS State by State Hotlines
www.thebody.com/hotlines/state.html

U.S. HIV/AIDS State by State Organizations
www.thebody.com/hotlines/other.html

Index

About the Author

Brette Sember is a retired attorney and author of 30 books, including *Gay & Lesbian Legal Rights: A GLBT Guide for Singles, Couples, and Families* (Sourcebooks, 2006), *Gay and Lesbian Parenting Choices: From Adopting or Using a Surrogate to Choosing the Perfect Father* (Career Press, 2006), *The Complete Gay Divorce* (Career Press, 2005), *Seniors' Rights: Your Legal Guide to Living Life to the Fullest* (Sourcebooks, 2006) and many more. She is a member of the American Society of Journalists and Authors (ASJA) and the Association of Health Care Journalists (AHCJ). Her Website is *www.BretteSember.com*.